24.3.00 Happy Birthday Dad
love Cath x x

IMAGES
of Sport

LEEDS UNITED FOOTBALL CLUB

The Leeds United squad, as seen by cartoonist 'Speed', that reached the FA Cup final for the first time in the club's history on 1 May 1965.

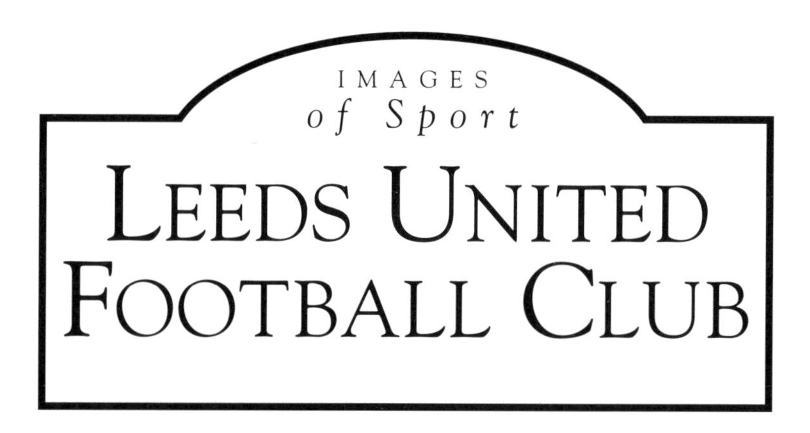

Compiled by

David Saffer and Howard Dapin

First published 1999
Reprinted 1999

Tempus Publishing Limited
The Mill, Brimscombe Port,
Stroud, Gloucestershire, GL5 2QG

ISBN 0 7524 1642 1

Typesetting and origination by
Tempus Publishing Limited
Printed in Great Britain by
Midway Clark Printing, Wiltshire

This book is dedicated to all Leeds United supporters, especially Daniella, Abigail & Jake Saffer and Sophie & Jade Dapin.

Acknowledgements

The authors would like to thank the following people and organisations for their help with this publication: Elsie Revie, Mike Fisher and Keith Hampshire at the *Yorkshire Evening Post*, Leeds United Football Club, James Howarth and Tony Lazenby. Finally, thanks to Deborah and Benita for their continued support and understanding!

Contents

Acknowledgements 4

Foreword 6

Introduction 7

Roll of Honour 8

1. Early Days: 1919-1939 9
2. The Rise of 'King John': 1946-1960 17
3. Glory, Glory, Leeds United: 1961-1974 31
4. Life after Don: 1975-1982 73
5. Wilderness Years: 1983-1988 85
6. 'Wilko': 1989-1996 91
7. The Move Towards Youth: 1997-1999 117

On 28 April 1974 Don Revie was a 'victim' of *This is Your Life*. A proud Elsie looks on as Don accepts the red book from host Eamonn Andrews at the Queens Hotel.

Foreword

Many of my fondest memories relate to the time Don and I lived in Leeds. Even when we moved away Don's heart remained there: in fact wherever we were in the world the first result he would look for was the Leeds one. I don't visit the city that often these days but when I do I'm overwhelmed by the good wishes I still receive. I suppose I shouldn't be surprised though, because throughout Don's time at the club the fans were always hugely supportive.

Don loved every minute of his time as manager. He and the coaching staff brought together a group of boys and watched them grow into men. Many are still friends, some are even grandfathers, but to me they will always be Don's 'boys'. It's often been said that the genuine affection Don and the 'boys' had for each other was a major reason why they were so successful. I agree, but another major factor was that the players Don was able to choose from were world class. In my view he created a team the like of which we'll never see again.

I am Honorary President of the Leeds United Supporters Club – a position I hold with pride and affection. They are a group of people who deserve success more than anyone for their devotion, and with David O'Leary in charge I'm sure that more glory is not that far away.

David and Howard have spent many hours researching this book and the finished result will fascinate the true Leeds United fans, whatever their age.

Elsie Revie
July 1999

Introduction

Like you, as Leeds supporters our lives have been affected by events at Elland Road and our allegiances date back to our first games –

David (Fairs Cup final, Leeds *v.* Ferencvaros, 7 August 1968): 'I was eight when my dad first took me to a game, but by the end I was hooked. I still recall the hubbub outside the ground, the atmosphere inside the Lowfields Road Stand, and the euphoria when Jones scored, as if it was yesterday. Three decades on, and many memories later, Dad has swapped his wooden seat for a comfy sofa, so I now follow the team's fortunes from the Family Stand with my son Jake, but I'll never forget that Ferencvaros game.'

Howard (Leeds *v.* Leicester, 12 March 1966): 'My father took me, a six-year old, to the Lowfields Road and recalls me sitting on the floor crying as City went two goals up. I was so upset; I just wanted to go home. Ignoring my pleas he told me to 'Shut up and watch'. I did, and with joyous astonishment watched United come back to win. Today, despite my wife and daughters having no interest whatsoever in football, I still experience the same feelings of despair and exhilaration, the only difference being I now sit on the West Stand floor and cry.'

Watching Revie's Leeds you went to a game wondering not if they would win, but by how many. The despondency of the '80s was overtaken by the renaissance under 'Wilko', whose finest hour at Bramall Lane was so strange it was as if someone was saying 'Here's your payback for the heartache and the what-might-have-beens you suffered in the past.'

This book covers the entire history of Leeds United, not just the football we witnessed. In it we describe the highs and lows and recall the achievements and personalities that shaped the club. Choosing just 226 images to sum up eighty years of Leeds United wasn't easy, but we hope you'll like the result.

Enjoy the memories,
David Saffer & Howard Dapin

Roll of Honour

Division One Champions
1968/69
1973/74
1991/92

Division Two Champions
1923/24
1963/64
1989/90

FA Cup
1972

Football League Cup
1968

Fairs Cup
1968
1971

FA Charity Shield
1969
1992

FA Youth Challenge Cup
1993
1997

One
Early Days
1919-1939

The boards of Leeds United and Bournemouth toast the King's health (January 1939). Seated in the centre of the front row is the club's first chairman, Mr Hilton Crowther – the man who did most to return league football to the city of Leeds after the demise of Leeds City.

Leeds United 1920/21. From left to right, back row: Barker, Crowther (chairman), Duffield, Cooper, Hart, Brown, Jacklin, Downs, Cooper, Walton, Jeffries, Stead (assistant manager), Fairclough (manager), Murrell (trainer). Middle row: Frew, Spencer, Lyons, Elson, Thompson, Stuart, Goldthorpe, Reynolds. Front row: Armitage, Mason, Baker (captain), Tillotson, Musgrove, McGee, Best. Leeds United's formation followed Leeds City's expulsion from the Football League for making illegal payments to players during the First World War. Managed initially by Dick Ray, the club was invited to join the Midland League on 31 October 1919. They drew their opening fixture with Barnsley Reserves 0-0 and had to wait until 20 December before registering their first victory, a 2-0 win over Lincoln City Reserves. The potential of the impoverished team attracted Hilton Crowther, the wealthy chairman of Huddersfield Town. Disillusioned by the lack of support in Huddersfield, Crowther sold his interest in Town to buy United and appointed Arthur Fairclough manager. Realising his long-term objectives could only be fulfilled if his team was elected to the Football League, Crowther used all his persuasive powers to help United win the annual poll and gain election to the Second Division on 31 May 1920. Leeds United's first League opponents were Port Vale (ironically the team that had replaced Leeds City) on 28 August 1920. Although Leeds lost 2-0, the return at Elland Road on 4 September brought United their first League victory by 3-1. In between, on 1 September, Len Armitage had scored United's first ever League goal against South Shields in a 2-1 defeat. Leeds finished the season comfortably in mid-table. From the beginning, Jim Baker and Bert Duffield had been mainstays in the side and both would play over 200 games for the club. Baker was United's first captain and led by example, while Duffield won few headlines but was vital in the centre of defence.

Leeds United 1923/24. From left to right, back row: Murrell (trainer), Bell, Coates, Robson, Armand, Menzies, Flood, Gordon, Noble, Duffield, Ure (assistant trainer). Third row: L. Baker, Frew, Smith, Hart, Morris, Bell, Swan, A. Baker, Gascoigne, Harris. Second row: Whalley, Johnson, Shirwin, Poyntz, Norman (team manager), Crowther, (chairman), Fairclough (secretary-manager), Richmond, Powell. Front row: Fullam, Down, Lambert, Mason, J. Baker (captain), Allen, Whipp, Speak. After two seasons of consolidation United were full of hope for the 1923/24 campaign, but made an unimpressive start. However, they soon improved, at one stage winning seven consecutive games. Confidence restored, goals began to flow through Swan, Richmond and Whipp. In a dramatic climax to the season United clinched their first honour, the Second Division championship, in the penultimate match against Nelson, Walter Coates scoring the only goal.

THE ONE OF TETLEY'S HOUSES

Whip Hotel

Briggate & Duncan Street

LEEDS

Most Central House in Leeds for Smoking Concerts, Meetings.

LEEDS UNITED

RIGHT — LEFT

Down

Duffield — Menzies

Baker, J. — Hart — Smith

Coates — Whipp — Richmond — Swan — Harris

Referee—
Mr. A. F. KIRBY

Linesmen—
Messrs. F. Hall & F. Burns.

Cameron — Wolstenholme — Edleston — Caulfield — Hoad

Wilson — Braidwood — Newnes

Rigg — Lilley, R.

Abbott

LEFT — RIGHT

NELSON

AN IDEAL DRINK

THE ROYAL YORKSHIRE

GINGER ALE (DRY or SWEET)

WITH A SLICE OF LEMON

AS SUPPLIED TO THE LEEDS UNITED FOOTBALL CLUB

Harston & Co., Ltd., Leeds (Tel. 27266) and Harrogate (Tel. 193.)

The team sheet from United's historic match against Nelson, 26 April 1924.

Tom Jennings was a goal-scoring phenomenon for Leeds, netting 117 goals in just 174 matches. Surviving a shipwreck on his way to the Canary Islands whilst at Raith Rovers, he joined the club in March 1925. In his first full season Jennings struck 26 goals, and in the relegation season that followed he scored 35 out of the team's total of 69. Although the campaign ended in bitter disappointment for the club, it was an incredible season for Jennings. Not only did he score four-tricks, but he also produced a scoring sequence that will probably never be bettered. In 9 games he scored 19 goals, in which 11 were scored in consecutive matches against Arsenal (3), Liverpool (4) and Blackburn (4). Top scorer between 1925/26 and 1927/28, his final tally would have been far greater had it not been for bouts of blood poisoning that restricted his appearances.

Charlie Keetley's career overlapped Jennings, and like his team-mate he had an amazing strike-rate, scoring 110 goals in 169 appearances. He was spotted whilst netting 80 goals in the 1926/27 season for Alvaston and Boulton, and joined Leeds in July 1927. In his debut season he scored on his first four appearances, including a hat-trick against Bristol City, and finished with 18 goals from only 16 appearances. During his Leeds career Keetley was top-scorer in 1928/29, 1930/31 and 1931/32, scored three hat-tricks in consecutive seasons (1927/28 and 1928/29) and is still the only player to score a hat-trick in six successive seasons (1927/28 to 1932/33).

Ernie Hart, signed at eighteen, proved to be an inspirational captain. A key member of the 1923/24 promotion-winning side, Hart was a solid defender who dealt uncompromisingly with opposing forwards. Although regarded as having a tough reputation, Hart was sent off just once in his career. He played 447 League games for Leeds and was capped 8 times by England.

Bobby Turnbull was a brilliant outside right and adored by Leeds fans. In his seven seasons with the club not only did he score 46 goals in 215 appearances, but also created countless others with his tricky wing play.

Left: Willis Edwards was destined to give Leeds many years' service. Signed from Chesterfield for £25,000 in 1925 he developed into one of the finest wing halves of his day and played 444 times. Edwards had everything: speed, control, strength, and stamina. He was also adept at creating chances for his colleagues with just one touch. Edwards was the first Leeds United player to represent England, in all winning 16 caps. *Right:* Bill Menzies joined Leeds in March 1922, and in a career that spanned nine years he played 258 games at left-back. Despite a skinny physique, his ability to 'read' the game and anticipate danger made him an indispensable part of Leeds' early defensive formation.

Below opposite: Leeds United 1929/30. From left to right, back row: Ray (manager), Reed, Hart, Potts, Milburn, Wilson, Jennings, Campbell (trainer). Front row: Turnbull, White, Edwards, Roberts, Wainscoat, Mitchell. The 1929/30 season was the best for Leeds since their formation; they even challenged for the title at New Year, winning seven consecutive games. Eventually though they finished fifth, a position not bettered for thirty-five years. At the heart of this success was the defensive partnership of Edwards and Hart, in front of either Bill Johnson or Jimmy Potts in goal. Potts played 262 games in all and was an imposing figure, arguably the best 'keeper to serve the club. Up front Russell Wainscoat top scored with 15 goals – in his six seasons he scored a total of 93 times in 226 games.

Following relegation in 1926/27 Arthur Fairclough resigned. Leeds replaced him with Dick Ray, who made an immediate impact. This League encounter against Chelsea on 10 December 1927 was one of many games during the 1927/28 season when Leeds simply couldn't stop scoring. In this 5-0 drubbing, Jennings scored four and White got the other goal. The season ended successfully with promotion to the First Division as runners-up with 57 points. In all Leeds scored 98 goals, scoring four or more goals on ten occasions.

Leeds United 1933/34. From left to right, back row: Hornby, George Milburn, Moore, Jones, Jack Milburn, Copping. Front row: Mahon, Roper, Hart, Keetley, Furness, Cochrane. Instead of building on their success in 1929/30, Leeds suffered one of their worst-ever seasons the following term and were relegated. The team responded magnificently in 1931/32 and, following a club record nine successive League victories, they were able to secure promotion as runners-up. Leeds stayed in the top flight for the rest of the decade. Their strength centred on the defence, which included the Milburn brothers, Edwards, Hart and Copping. This enabled strikers Furness, Cochrane and Hydes to attack freely. Wilf Copping was the original 'hard man', he was a rock and no one frightened him. He was idolised by fans and played 183 games before moving to Arsenal where he won every domestic honour. He was capped 20 times by England. Jack Milburn missed only a handful of games throughout his career, eventually playing 408 matches. He still holds a club record for scoring nine penalties in the 1935/36 season. Younger brother George didn't have the same success but partnered Jack at full-back on 166 occasions. Tom Cochrane and Billy Furness formed a wonderful partnership on the left flank, amassing 259 and 257 appearances respectively. Furness was the superior goalscorer with 66 but couldn't match the phenomenal scoring rate of Arthur Hydes, who struck 82 goals in 137 games. In all Hydes was top-scorer in four campaigns, three of them consecutive (1933-35). During this period Hydes missed (through injury) the 8-0 demolition of Leicester on 7 April 1934, United's record League victory. The club's status in the 1930s was only tested in 1936/37 when they gained just three points away from home, but thirty-four year old Gordon Hodgson, a scoring machine from South Africa, saved them. Having scored 233 goals in 258 League appearances for Liverpool, he struck 53 for Leeds in 86 games, including a club-record five in United's 8-2 defeat of Leicester on 1 October 1938. The 1938/39 season was the last full season before the Second World War and Leeds finished thirteenth.

Two

The Rise of 'King John' 1946-1960

John Charles, Roy Wood and Keith Ripley, together with their wives, enjoy a social evening held at the ROF Sports Club, Barnbow. The event was organized by the Cross Gates and Halton branch of Leeds United Supporters' Club, November 1956.

The war years affected Leeds more than most teams as their ageing side struggled to reach the standards they had previously achieved. In a disastrous initial campaign Leeds gained just six victories and one away point all season. Unsurprisingly they finished bottom with 18 points, an unwanted club record. Willis Edwards (above) replaced Billy Hampson as manager, but Edwards only lasted a season as the slide continued and was himself succeeded by Major Frank Buckley in May 1948.

Right-back Jimmy Dunn represented Leeds on 443 occasions. Unlucky to miss out on international honours for Scotland, he added strength and security to the right flank. He missed only eighteen games in ten seasons.

Tommy Burnden was a magnificent signing by Buckley in 1948. This remarkable wing half made 259 appearances and remained totally committed despite commuting from the West Country during his seven seasons. An inspirational skipper and motivator, he missed only a handful of matches before moving to Bristol City in 1954.

Eric Kerfoot played 349 times for Leeds. A dynamic wing half, he became captain after Burnden left. Kerfoot led the club in the 1955/56 promotion campaign.

Harold Williams joined Leeds in 1949 and was equally effective on either wing. He was deceptive, resilient and quick. A Welsh international, he made 228 appearances during his six-year spell.

Leeds United 1949/50. From left to right, back row: Charles, Kerfoot, Dunn, Dudley, Searson, Milburn. Front row: Cochrane, Iggledon, Burnden, Browning, Williams. In 1949/50 United finished fifth in the Second Division and reached the sixth round of the FA Cup for the first time. Defensive frailties were reduced to a minimum with Jim Milburn (nearing the end of his seventeen-year stay), Dunn, Kerfoot, Burnden and John Charles forming a solid barrier. However, it was the strikers that really caught the eye. David Cochrane, capped by Northern Ireland, was a 'wizard' on the ball. The fans' anticipation grew every time he had possession and in thirteen seasons he made 185 appearances. Ray Iggledon was top-scorer in 1951/52 and eventually struck 50 goals in 181 appearances. Iggledon could play in either inside position but was most dangerous on the left where he combined with Williams. Completing the forward line was Len Browning, top-scorer in 1948/49 and 1950/51. Browning was surprisingly transfer listed at the end of the 1950/51 season and it was a puzzle at the time why a player with the best strike-rate since Arthur Hydes (46 goals in 105 appearances) was allowed to leave his hometown club.

Granville Hair's 474 games straddled United's old and modern era. Signed by Major Buckley, he also played under four other managers. A brilliant left-back, his main attributes were speed, strength, and anticipation. After making his debut in 1950 he was first choice until handing over to Willie Bell at the start of the 1963/64 season. Though he never played for England, he did represent the FA on trips to Africa, New Zealand, and the West Indies.

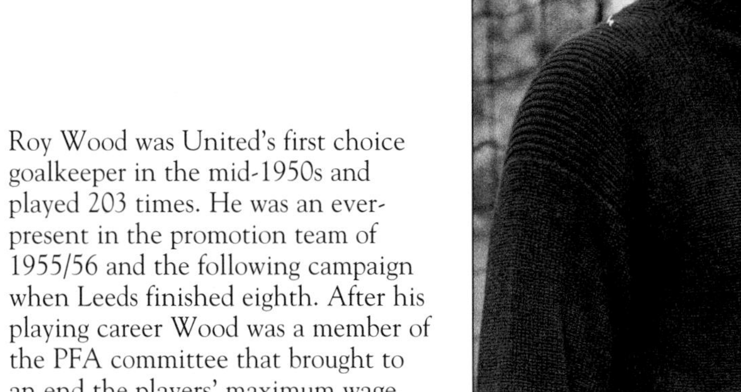

Roy Wood was United's first choice goalkeeper in the mid-1950s and played 203 times. He was an ever-present in the promotion team of 1955/56 and the following campaign when Leeds finished eighth. After his playing career Wood was a member of the PFA committee that brought to an end the players' maximum wage.

Leeds United 1955/56. From left to right, back row: Kerfoot, Dunn, Marsden, Scott, Burnden, Hair. Front row: Williams, Vickers, Charles, Nightingale, McCall. The 'Major' stabilised Leeds in the top ten but the board wanted promotion and appointed Raich Carter manager in 1953. In his first season Leeds finished tenth, Charles scoring a club record 42 League goals. The following term United missed promotion by just a point, with Charles plundering goals consistently. It was third time lucky in 1955/56 as Leeds won their last six matches to finish runners-up behind Sheffield Wednesday. Charles was once again the star, starting the campaign in defence he moved forward when Jack Charlton broke into the first team and scored 29 times.

Albert Nightingale was Leed's answer to Clark Gable! A £10,000 signing from Blackburn in 1952, he was an exciting inside forward who linked well with Charles and liked nothing better than running at a defence with the ball at his feet. Nightingale played 135 games, scoring 48 goals.

John Charles shakes hands with brother Mel before the League clash with Swansea Town on 11 February 1956. The match ended 2-2 with Charles and Nightingale scoring the Leeds goals.

Leeds defeated Bristol Rovers 2-1 on 21 April 1956, their last home game of the season, before an ecstatic crowd of over 49,000. Here, John Charles is pictured scoring the opening goal.

Rotherham goalkeeper Reg Quairney gathers a cross before Charles can pounce in the penultimate match of the season on 23 April 1956. Two Nightingale strikes won the points for Leeds.

Around 31,000 fans packed Hull City's ground on 28 April 1956 to witness United clinch promotion. Leeds ran out easy winners with Charles and Brook both scoring twice in the 4-1 victory.

Leeds United 1956/57. From left to right, back row: Kerfoot, Ripley, Dunn, Wood, Hair, Charlton. Front row: Meek, Nightingale, Charles, Brook, Overfield. United's first season back in the top flight surprised many – well organised and consistent they finished eighth. Although eight of the squad made at least 40 appearances, nobody could argue that Charles was the key player. The club was well aware that teams throughout Europe were watching him, and another 38 League goals meant they could no longer hang on to their most prized asset. Juventus tabled a world record bid of £65,000 and the club had no option but to accept; Charles left at the end of the season.

During the early hours of 18 September 1956 a fire swept through the West Stand. The fire brigade were unable to prevent the roof collapsing and destroying the club's offices, dressing rooms, press box and medical centre. A few days later Charles led his men out through the charred remains before scoring the only goal in a 1-0 victory over Aston Villa. If you look closely, his burned number 8 shirt can be seen draped over a piece of steel.

Charles in action against Birmingham City twenty-five days after the stand fire.

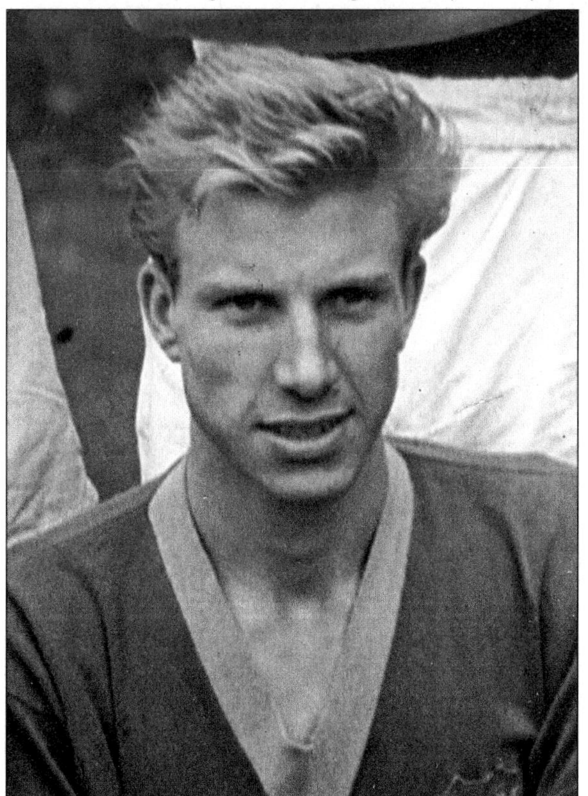

Left: Jack Overfield made his debut in the 1955/56 promotion season and went on to play 163 games, scoring 20 goals. *Right:* George Meek played 199 games during an eight-year stay that saw him in and out of the side due to national service. Though not prolific scorers, both these wingers provided many opportunities for their colleagues.

A legend: John Charles made his debut for Leeds in 1948/49 at seventeen years old. Impregnable in defence and unstoppable in attack, he scored 157 goals in 327 appearances. Charles was Leeds' top scorer in 1952/53, 1953/54, 1955/56, and 1956/57. It is unlikely that his club record of 42 League goals in the 1953/54 season will ever be bettered. He was worshipped at Juventus where he won League and cup medals, and was named Italian Player of the Year. After making his debut for Wales at eighteen he went on to win 38 caps and was outstanding during the 1958 World Cup.

The players and the United programme were utilized to raise funds after the fire. *Above:* In April 1957, the club allowed training sessions to be filmed and shown at local cinemas. Extreme left is Jerry Francis (United's first black player), whilst John Charles and Raich Carter are on the right. Jack Charlton is in the centre. *Right:* United advertise for benefactors in their match programme for the game against Luton Town on 9 February 1957.

"SILVER" TICKETS

Your own Seat ANYWHERE on the New Stand each year for

TWENTY YEARS

(SUBJECT TO ENTERTAINMENT TAX)

YOU can still sit next to your friends

even if they do not have a "SILVER" TICKET

DON'T FORGET, the Ticket is TRANSFERABLE

IMMEDIATE APPLICATION with cheque for 100 guineas

or enquiries to

J. L. BRILL
c/o J. L. BRILL, LTD.
32 BOND STREET, LEEDS 1

C. SIMON
c/o BENJAMIN SIMON & SONS, LTD.
PARK LANE, LEEDS 1

Dr. WINDER
THORNER LODGE
THORNER, near LEEDS

Help the Club and yourself by applying at once

When Raich Carter's contract wasn't renewed in May 1958 Leeds appointed Bill Lambton as manager. The most significant contribution Lambton made, before being replaced by Jack Taylor, was the signing of Don Revie from Sunderland for £12,000. Nobody could envisage the outcome this acquisition would have on the club. In his playing career for Leeds Revie scored 12 goals in 80 appearances. He is captured here trying to force the ball past West Brom goalkeeper Potter. United's form after Charles' departure was poor, and after hovering for two seasons above the relegation zone they finally dropped into the Second Division at the end of the 1959/60 season.

Three

Glory, Glory, Leeds United 1961-1974

Leeds United 1961/62. From left to right, back row: Owen (coach), Cocker (trainer), Hawksby, Humphreys, Kilford, Charlton, Thompson, Addy, Sprake, Metcalfe, Reaney, Johnson, English (physiotherapist), Revie (manager). Middle row: Bremner, Francis, Mayers, Smith, Hallet, Carling, Johanneson, Bell. Front row: Hunter, Casey, Hair, Jones, Ryden, McCole, Cameron, Grainger, Peyton, McConnell, Cooper. It is well documented that Revie's appointment as manager, four days after Jack Taylor's resignation, followed approaches from Bournemouth and Chester. Harry Reynolds, whilst writing a reference, realised Revie was the man Leeds needed, so promptly offered him the post. This squad picture was taken just before Revie's first season in charge, which saw Leeds avoid relegation on the last day of the campaign with a 3-0 victory at St James Park. In a season when Leeds struggled to score, Bremner and Charlton ended joint top scorers with 12 goals each. It is ironic that the club's lowest ever League position should come in Revie's first season as manager.

Joining Revie from left to right are: Harold Williamson (general manager), Harry Reynolds (chairman), Bob English (physiotherapist), Les Cocker (trainer), and Syd Owen (coach). In fifteen years this group turned Leeds United from a club struggling to achieve mediocrity into one of the most feared club sides in Europe.

Members of United's board await the start of 1964 AGM. From left to right: Morris, Bolton, Reynolds, Woodward, Marjason and Simon. Don Revie was not the only man who had a vision for Leeds United. The contribution made by the chairman, Harry Reynolds, is often overlooked. If he hadn't spotted the managerial potential in Revie who knows what direction the club's future may have taken?

'Silitex' HOSIERY AND LINGERIE
FOR SATISFACTION FROM ALL LEADING DRAPERS

SATURDAY, APRIL 11, 1964
No. 22,882
Tel. Leeds 32701

YORKSHIRE
EVENING POST

Incorporating the YORKSHIRE EVENING NEWS
PRINTED SIMULTANEOUSLY IN LEEDS AND DONCASTER

Price 3d.

Peacock does 'em proud with 2 goals in 4 minutes

UP GO UNITED!

And the last time we said UP GO UNITED was April 28, 1956

RESULTS

Giles nets another

THEY'VE made it! Leeds United clinched their promotion to Division 1 when they grabbed the two necessary points by beating Swansea today and set the champagne flowing.

By PHIL BROWN

At SWANSEA

SWANSEA TOWN.—Dwyer; R. Evans, Roy Hughes; Johnson, Purcell, Williams; Jones, Draper, Thomas, McLaughlin, Bryan Evans.

LEEDS UNITED.—Sprake; Reaney, Bell; Bremner, Charlton, Hunter; Giles, Weston, Peacock, Collins, Cooper.

Referee. Mr. N. A. S. Matthews (Bicester).

Hull KR and Oldham must battle again

DONOVAN (white shirt), the Oldham centre, is brought down by Burwell and Elliott of Hull K.R.

DROPPED GOAL SQUARES GAME

The *Yorkshire Evening Post* report on United's 3-0 defeat of Swansea on 11 April 1964. This win brought Revie's first success – promotion to Division One. Leeds ended the season as champions with 63 points. United scored 71 goals during the campaign, despite having Jim Storrie, top scorer the previous season, struggling for fitness. Johanneson and Weston scored 13, but it was mid-season signing Alan Peacock who acted as the catalyst for promotion, scoring 8 goals in just 14 appearances.

Leeds parading the Second Division trophy through the city before a civic reception at the Town Hall. Captain Bobby Collins, a £25,000 acquisition from Everton, was the first of three small Scottish midfielders who would have a miraculous effect on the club's fortunes. In all he made 167 appearances for Leeds, scoring 25 goals.

Leeds United, 1964/65. From left to right, back row: Bell, Hunter, Reaney, Charlton, Greenhoff, Cooper. Middle row: Owen (coach), Peacock, Weston, Sprake, Revie (manager), Williamson, Madeley, Wright, English (physiotherapist). Front row: Bremner, Giles, Storrie, Collins, Henderson, Weston, Johnson. This remarkable squad came agonisingly close to the 'double' on their return to the top flight. Revie's disciplined, well-organized team developed a fierce reputation that received much media criticism. Unperturbed, they only lost the title to Manchester United on goal difference and the FA Cup in extra-time to Liverpool.

Cup fever! After defeating Southport, Everton, Shrewsbury and Crystal Palace, Leeds faced Manchester United in the semi-finals at Hillsborough. Here, supporters queue outside Lowfield Road for tickets – if only we could have those prices again! In an epic semi-final, which went to a replay, Bremner headed the only goal with just 2 minutes remaining.

The *Yorkshire Evening Post* FA Cup final souvenir paper to commemorate United's big day on April 26 1965.

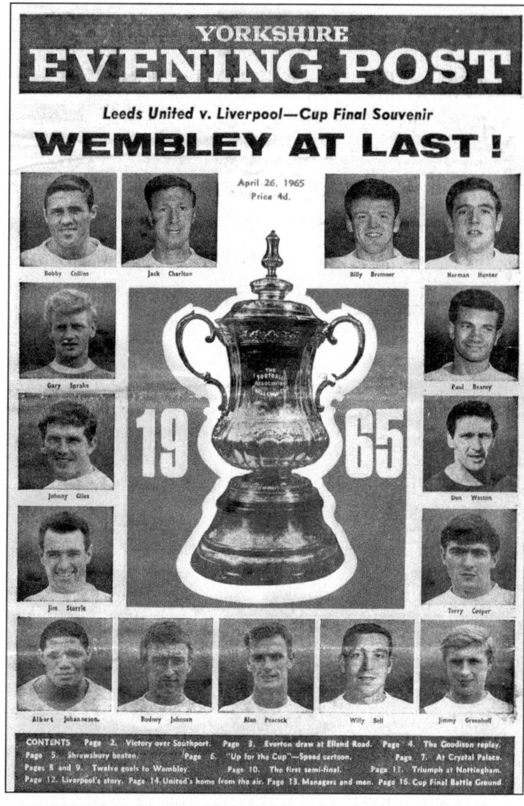

YORKSHIRE
EVENING POST

Leeds United v. Liverpool—Cup Final Souvenir

WEMBLEY AT LAST!

April 26, 1965
Price 4d.

Bobby Collins
Jack Charlton
Billy Bremner
Norman Hunter
Gary Sprake
Paul Reaney
Johnny Giles
Don Weston
Jim Storrie
Terry Cooper

19 65

Albert Johanneson.
Rodney Johnson
Alan Peacock
Willy Bell
Jimmy Greenhoff

CONTENTS Page 2. Victory over Southport. Page 3. Everton draw at Elland Road. Page 4. The Goodison replay. Page 5. Shrewsbury beaten. Page 6. "Up for the Cup"—Speed cartoon. Page 7. At Crystal Palace. Pages 8 and 9. Twelve goals to Wembley. Page 10. The first semi-final. Page 11. Triumph at Nottingham. Page 12. Liverpool's story. Page 14. United's home from the air. Page 13. Managers and men. Page 16. Cup Final Battle Ground.

Leeds United's 1965 FA Cup final side. From left to right, back row: Hunter, Charlton, Sprake, Reaney, Bell. Front row: Giles, Storrie, Peacock, Revie (manager), Collins, Johanneson, Bremner. On their first visit to Wembley Leeds struggled throughout. Bremner's strike in extra-time was the only highlight in a 2-1 defeat.

Despite the FA Cup final disappointment, thousands of fans welcomed their team home.

The team's achievements, in what was to turn out to be a breakthrough season, deserved and received a civic reception. Here Alderman Naylor, the Lord Mayor, acts as the representative of a proud city.

Crowd trouble in September 1966 mars United's clash with Everton. Meetings between these sides in the mid-1960s were fierce encounters in which no prisoners were taken. By far the worst moment occurred at Goodison in 1964 when the referee stopped the match to allow both teams to cool down following numerous incidents, including the sending off of an Everton player. Leeds eventually won the match with a goal from Willie Bell. A strong-tackling left-back, Bell played 260 matches during Revie's early years before losing his place to Terry Cooper in 1968.

On 29 September 1965, Revie's dream of pitting his wits against the best in Europe became reality when Leeds played Torino in the Fairs Cup. Peacock is pictured heading home the winning goal in United's 2-1 victory. Leeds reached the semi-finals before losing to Real Zaragoza on aggregate.

Peter 'Hot-shot' Lorimer fires home during United's 5-0 FA Cup victory over West Brom in 1967. Lorimer was a prodigious goalscorer and provider of goals. After making his debut in 1962 at 15 years and 289 days old (still a club record), he went on to play 703 games, scoring a club record 238 goals. He was top scorer in 1965/66, 1967/68 and 1971/72.

Why were Leeds on the wrong end of so many controversial decisions in the late '60s and early '70s? Here, in the 1967 FA Cup semi-final against Chelsea, Cooper (11) Giles and Greenhoff (9) surround the referee after Lorimer's last minute free kick was disallowed by referee Ken Burns because it was taken too quickly! Chelsea couldn't believe their luck and clung on to win 1-0.

Leeds' 1966/67 Fairs Cup campaign started with a comfortable 8-2 aggregate win over DWS Amsterdam. Albert Johanneson is shown here scoring in the home leg. A remarkable talent, Johanneson overcame racial taunts to star for Leeds in 200 games, scoring 67 goals. His wonderful skills enabled him to mesmerise opponents, but a combination of injury and the emergence of Eddie Gray ended the South African's United career.

You didn't have to defeat the opposition or take penalties to win in Europe in the 1960s: Billy Bremner celebrates victory over Bologna in 1967 after calling correctly on the toss of a coin after the sides drew on aggregate.

Rod Belfitt scores one of his three goals against Kilmarnock in United's Fairs Cup semi-final clash at Elland Road on 19 May 1967. Leeds held on to their 4-2 advantage in the return leg to reach their first European final.

It is August 1967 and Bremner leads out his side for the first leg of the 1967 Fairs Cup final against Dynamo Zagreb. Without Giles, Bell, Madeley and Johanneson, United lost 2-0. In the return leg at Elland Road United's inexperience in Europe was apparent as Zagreb comfortably held on to their advantage.

Match programme for Arsenal *v.* Leeds United in the 1968 Football League Cup final.

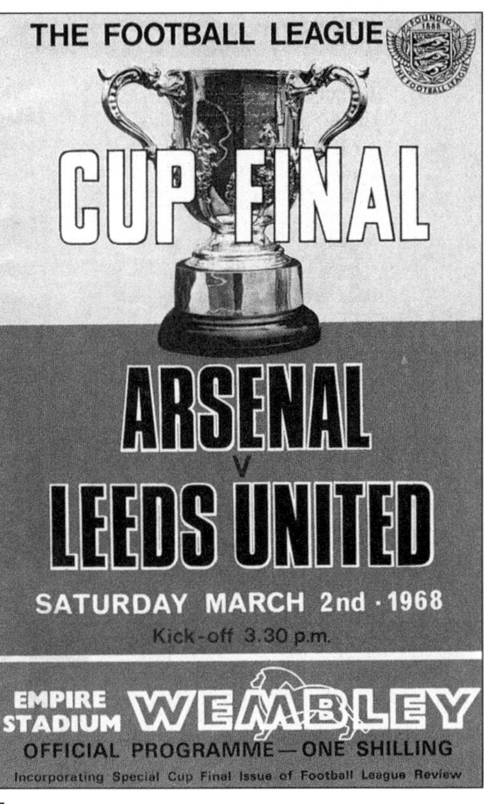

The League Cup final, 2 March 1968. Revie and Cocker celebrate at the final whistle. The hero that day was Terry Cooper, whose first half strike was sufficient for Leeds to defeat Arsenal. The trophy-winning team consisted of: Sprake, Reaney, Cooper, Bremner, Charlton, Hunter, Greenhoff, Lorimer, Madeley, Giles, Gray, Belfitt (substitute).

HENNEBIQUE READY MIXED CONCRETE

SATURDAY MARCH 2, 1968

YORKSHIRE EVENING POST

SPORTS ECHO

LARGEST CIRCULATION IN THE LARGEST COUNTY

Price 5d

OMEGA

Blow for Gunners in £100,000 final

COOPER HITS DREAM GOAL

FOOTBALL RESULTS

Gray hurt but carries on

WEMBLEY LINE-UP

Bottles hurled at Leeds fans' coach

Double for Britain

THIS SUNDAY 9am till 2pm at WHITEHALL TRADE WAREHOUSE

DISPOSAL OF ENTIRE CENTRAL HEATING STOCKS

BRANDED KITCHENS LESS UP TO 33⅓%

58 WHITEHALL RD. LEEDS 12

The front page of the *Yorkshire Evening Post 'Sports Echo'* edition, 2 March 1968. Note that the football results section only has the half-time score from Wembley as the main copy was printed before the end of the game. The final result appeared in the late results section on the back page.

After their League Cup triumph United almost became the first team to reach both domestic cup finals in the same season, but lost to Everton in the FA Cup semi-finals. This cartoon by 'Speed' appeared in the build-up to United's sixth round clash with Sheffield United, which was won by a single Paul Madeley goal.

Bremner and Grieg exchange pennants before their sides' Fairs Cup quarter-final clash, 16 March 1968. In an intense first leg contest at Ibrox, Leeds were the happier after the 0-0 draw. Second leg goals by Giles and Lorimer took United through to the semi-finals, where they overcame Dundee 2-1 on aggregate.

Match programme for Leeds United *v.* Ferencvaros, Fairs Cup final first leg, 7 August 1968.

Mick Jones ends up in the back of the net after scrambling home the only goal of the match against Ferencvaros of Hungary in the Fairs Cup final first leg.

On a night of unbearable tension at the Nep Stadium in the second leg game, Leeds somehow held on to a 0-0 draw to clinch their first European trophy. The defence, Sprake in particular, performed heroics. This was one of United's greatest displays in Europe, and afterwards Revie commented, 'When we got into those final few minutes my heart nearly stopped beating. As the final whistle drew nearer every minute seemed like an hour.' Bremner, held by Charlton and Sprake, is pictured here showing off the Fairs Cup, 11 September 1968.

United relax after defeating Ferencvaros.

After going so close for a number of seasons Leeds finally had silverware to show off. The squad are pictured here proudly displaying the Football League Cup and the Fairs Cup in September 1968. From left to right, back row: Reaney, Charlton, Madeley, Jones, Harvey, Sprake, Belfitt, Gray, Hunter. Front row: Hibbit, Giles, Cooper, Bremner, O'Grady, Bates, Lorimer, Johanneson.

Champions at last! 28 April 1969 was a historic night for Leeds as they clinched the First Division title for the first time in their history following a 0-0 draw with Liverpool. The glory of this occasion was enhanced by the sporting reaction of the Liverpool 'Kop' who insisted the team perform a lap of honour. Already Football League Champions, Leeds won their final game against Nottingham Forest thanks to a single Giles strike. After the match Bremner was presented with the Championship trophy before 46,500 ecstatic fans.

Another civic reception, but this time Leeds fans celebrate winning the premier domestic competition. In a remarkable campaign, Leeds amassed 67 points and lost only twice (both Division One records at the time). In addition, club records included most home wins (18), and least goals conceded both at home (9) and overall (26). With such defensive superiority the 66 league goals shared throughout the squad was more than sufficient, Jones top-scoring with 14.

This *Yorkshire Evening Post* special souvenir commemorated United's League triumph in April 1969.

The Leeds United squad as seen by cartoonist 'Speed', April 1969.

By 1969/70 Leeds were at their peak and all the first-team players were full internationals. From left to right: Lorimer (Scotland), Charlton (England), Clarke (England), Jones (England), Gray (Scotland), Madeley (England), Cooper (England), Hunter (England), Giles (Eire), Reaney (England), Sprake (Wales), Bremner (Scotland).

United played in the European Cup for the first time in August 1969. 'Speed' was certainly confident!

Sprake and Cooper clear their lines. Gary Sprake played 506 games for Leeds and it is unfortunate that his crucial mistakes are talked about more than his many consistent displays. Terry Cooper was a world class left-back, acknowledged as the best in the 1970 World Cup. He played 350 matches but a horrific leg injury shortly before the 1972 Cup Final effectively ended his Leeds career. Cooper will always be remembered for scoring the only goal of the 1968 League Cup final.

Carpet bowls was a popular distraction for the players during the build-up to a game. Here Clarke targets the jack as Giles, Hunter, Charlton and Cooper plan their strategy.

In the summer of 1969 Leeds paid a record British transfer fee of £165,000 for Allan 'Sniffer' Clarke. Top scorer in 1970/71, 1972/73 and 1974/75, and jointly with Jones in 1969/70, Clarke was probably the most clinical finisher ever to play for Leeds. He also had an uncanny ability to always be in the right place and rarely missed out when 'one-on-one' with the goalkeeper. Clarke scored the most famous goal in the club's history in the 1972 Cup Final, and went on to play 364 games, scoring 151 goals. He is shown here slotting home one of his four goals in United's 6-0 demolition of Sutton United in an FA Cup fourth round tie, January 1970.

In United's 1969/70 FA Cup run, Clarke scored seven times, including this sixth round effort against Swindon in February 1970.

This 'Speed' cartoon appeared in the build-up to Leeds' FA Cup semi-final clash with Manchester United in March 1970.

Leeds eventually reached their second FA Cup final thanks to a Bremner goal in the second replay at Burnden Park, Bolton. Here Clarke and Jones congratulate their skipper as Charlton, Lorimer and Cooper rush to join them, 26 March 1970.

The *Yorkshire Evening Post* FA Cup final souvenir special, April 1970. When this was published the 'treble' was still a possibility.

The United squad pose during the build-up to the 1970 FA Cup final. From left to right, back row: Reaney, Sprake, Harvey, Cooper. Middle row: Bremner, Hunter, Charlton, Madeley, Yorath. Front row: Gray, Lorimer, Giles, Bates, Clarke, Jones, Hibbit, Belfitt. A formidable squad, Leeds played 62 games during the season, scoring 127 goals. The front three of Lorimer, Clarke and Jones contributed 71 goals between them.

The FA Cup final, on 11 April 1970, was played at the end of a hectic twenty-nine day period when the FA forced Leeds to play eleven vital matches. Following heavy rain and the Horse of the Year Show, Wembley was a disgrace. However, Eddie Gray (left) overcame these conditions to give a virtuoso performance, deservedly winning the Man of the Match award. Unfortunately it proved insufficient as a Sprake 'howler' and a late equaliser gave Chelsea an undeserved replay. Eddie Gray was quite simply a magician – the most naturally gifted player to represent Leeds, his sublime dribbling skills mesmerised opposing defences. In a career spoiled by injury he played 578 games and scored 68 goals, none better than his solo effort against Burnley in 1970 which is arguably the best ever United goal. Eddie is one of a rare breed of talented footballers who can pass on their vast knowledge to generations that follow. Today United benefit from his services as one of the most influential coaches in the modern game.

The replay was a bruising affair that the Londoners edged 2-1 after extra time. It was a bitterly disappointing end to the season for Leeds. Fatigue, caused by fixture congestion, was a major factor why they missed out on any success, let alone the 'treble'. Whilst many outside the club were sympathetic it was little consolation to a distraught set of players. Here, Revie gives his players their final instructions before extra time.

One player who missed out on the end of season drama was Paul Reaney, who broke his leg at West Ham a week before the Cup Final. However, Reaney fought back and was playing again by October. He played 746 games at right-back in a career that lasted seventeen seasons. An England international, who Billy Bremner recalled as being 'so bloody quick', he had an incredible ability to recover and make last ditch tackles. He was also noted for his goal-line clearances, most famously in the 1972 Cup Final.

A Geordie, Norman 'Bites your legs' Hunter was Leeds through and through. He had a fierce reputation for sheer hardness, however this belied the skills of an extremely talented defender who graced United's side on 724 occasions. Capped 28 times by England, Hunter was voted the first ever PFA Player of the Year in 1973.

Lorimer hits one of his goals against Huddersfield in a 2-0 win on 3 October 1970.United started the 1970/71 season in determined fashion, losing just once in twenty-four League games.

Paul Madeley scores a rare goal in a 3-1 victory over Blackpool on 14 November 1970. Known as 'Mr Versatile', Madeley was invaluable, playing in every outfield position during his career. Capped 24 times by England, he was never recognised as having a regular position at the club but always figured in Revie's line-ups, whether for injury, suspension or tactical reasoning. In all he scored 34 times in 724 appearances.

During the run-in to the 1970/71 season United lost a seven point advantage in the Championship. The lead finally disappeared when they entertained West Brom on 17 April 1971. Just after half-time, with Leeds a goal down, Tony Brown intercepted Hunter's pass and broke across the half-way line. The linesman immediately raised his flag for offside as Suggett was returning from a previous attack. The Leeds players and Brown stopped but referee Tinkler waved play on. Brown carried the ball forward before squaring it to Astle, who (looking suspiciously offside) side-footed the ball into an empty net. The crowd erupted, fans invaded the pitch and the Leeds players and Revie protested, but the referee was adamant and the goal stood. Clarke's late goal was a mere consolation and Arsenal went on to clinch the title by a point. In this photograph, Tinkler watches Cocker treat a linesman who'd been hit by a missile. Tinkler required a police escort at the finish.

Happily, United were cruising through the Fairs Cup competition in 1970/71. Having disposed of Sarpsborg 6-0 on aggregate and Dynamo Dresdon on away goals, Leeds brushed aside Sparta Prague 9-2 on aggregate. Victory over Victoria Setubal set up a semi-final clash with Liverpool. Here, Bremner heads the only goal of the tie in the first leg at Anfield. United were through to their third Fairs Cup final where they would face Italian giants Juventus.

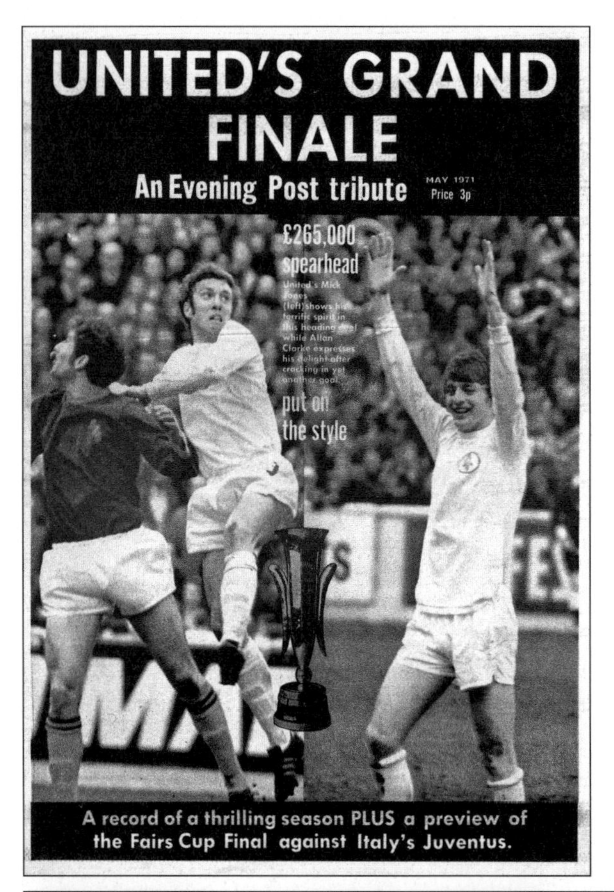

UNITED'S GRAND FINALE

An Evening Post tribute

MAY 1971
Price 3p

£265,000 spearhead

United's Mick Jones (left) shows his terrific spirit in this heading duel while Allan Clarke expresses his delight after cracking in yet another goal.

put on the style

A record of a thrilling season PLUS a preview of the Fairs Cup Final against Italy's Juventus.

The *Yorkshire Evening Post* brought out this souvenir paper to mark United's appearance in the Fairs Cup final, May 1971.

Players and officials on both United and Juventus benches shelter from incessant rain in the Fairs Cup final first leg, 28 May 1971. Torrential downpours made football impossible and the game was eventually abandoned after 53 minutes. When the match was replayed a couple of days later United twice came from behind to record a magnificent 2-2 result, with goals from Madeley and Bates. Mick Bates scored 9 goals in 187 appearances during his ten-year spell, but was never a regular. Despite this, both players and fans alike appreciated his unselfish role as the perennial substitute.

Clarke fires home the opening goal of the second leg against Juventus at Elland Road on 2 June 1971. Although Anastasi equalised it was not enough to prevent United taking the trophy on the away goals rule.

United after their victory over Juventus.

At times during the 1971/72 season Leeds played a standard of football that opponents could only dream about. Two displays in particular stood out, both of which were covered by *Match of the Day*. Firstly, on 19 February, Leeds hammered Manchester United 5-1 with Mick Jones scoring a hat-trick. Two weeks later they annihilated Southampton 7-0 with Lorimer scoring a hat-trick. The quality of play against Southampton was unbelievable, in particular a passing sequence towards the end when Leeds simply toyed with their opponents. Both displays helped to erase a general perception that Leeds were only a hard, workmanlike and aggressive side. *Above*: Jones scores one of his second half goals against Manchester United. *Below*: Lorimer crashes home one of his, past a dispirited Southampton defence.

In a bid to help their public image the team performed pre-match callisthenics a few minutes before kick-off and wore stocking tabs, which they gave to fans at the final whistle. Jones is pictured giving his tags to a delighted supporter after a 3-0 victory over Arsenal.

Determined to overcome the embarrassment of the Colchester FA Cup defeat the previous season, United progressed to a tricky fifth round tie at Cardiff's Ninian Park. The photograph shows Giles scoring one of his goals in a comfortable 2-0 win. Johnny Giles replaced Bobby Collins at the heart of United's midfield in the mid-1960s. A master at reading a game and spreading play, he developed a telepathic understanding with Bremner. During their partnership they became one of the most effective and feared midfield combinations in Europe. Giles scored 115 goals in 525 appearances and was capped 32 times by Eire.

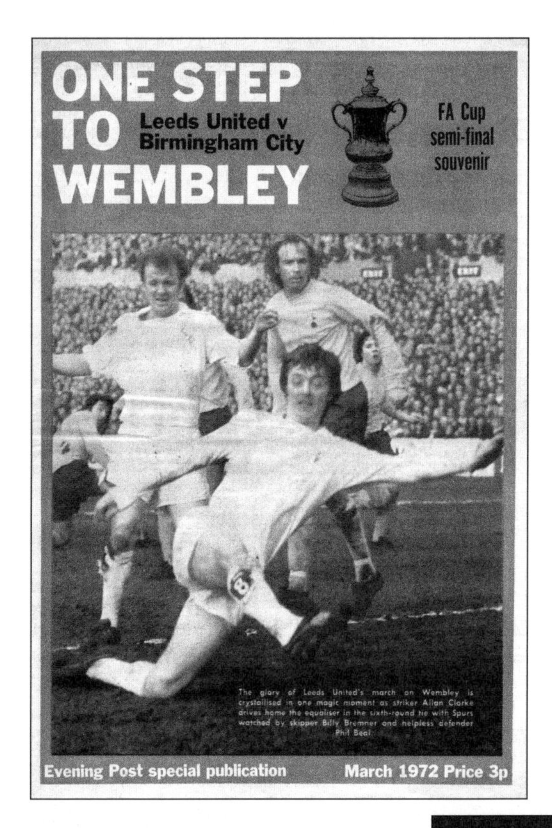
ONE STEP TO WEMBLEY

Leeds United v Birmingham City

FA Cup semi-final souvenir

The glory of Leeds United's march on Wembley is crystallised in one magic moment as striker Allan Clarke drives home the equaliser in the sixth-round tie with Spurs watched by skipper Billy Bremner and helpless defender Phil Beal.

Evening Post special publication March 1972 Price 3p

After overcoming Tottenham 2-1 in the sixth round, Leeds were drawn against Second Division Birmingham City in the semi-finals. This match was the turning point in David Harvey's career at Leeds. Following a number of solid performances, Revie made him 'keeper in preference to a fit-again Sprake. Harvey went on to play 446 games for Leeds. Within months he was capped by Scotland and went on to be voted the best goalkeeper at the 1974 World Cup.

United breezed into their third FA Cup final, defeating Birmingham 3-0. Here, Jones is pictured celebrating one of his brace of goals with Clarke. Jones was a non-stop battler, a braveheart, and never believed anything was a lost cause. He struck 111 goals in 312 appearances, top-scoring in 1968/69, 1973/74 and, jointly with Clarke, in 1969/70. He was the ideal partner for Clarke's mercurial talent and silky skills.

The *Yorkshire Evening Post* Centenary Cup Final publication, April 1972.

Below left: Match programme for Arsenal *v.* Leeds United, 1972 FA Cup final.
Below right: Saturday evening's *Green Post*, 6 May 1972, was the first local paper to report on United's FA Cup success.

GREEN POST

IT'S YOURS, UNITED

£5,000 and car in Pick the Spot

Free transfer for cup hero and Storrie

Clarke header brings Cup to Elland Road: 1-0

Reaney 'rescue act' yet again

Conteh sprints to hat-trick

Death ends family Cup Final plan

Cricket scores

Aussie Soccer Results

At last! Billy Bremner gets his hands on the FA Cup after a diving header from Clarke on 53 minutes, after a typically strong surging run by Jones, proved sufficient to bring United victory. Bremner arrived at Elland Road in 1959, making his debut a year later. Though only 5 feet 5 inches tall he played like a giant. After overcoming homesickness in the early days he became skipper of the side throughout their glory years. He had everything – fitness, speed, guts and style. He was a ball-winner one minute and a goalscorer the next. Bremner struck 155 goals in 771 appearances for Leeds United. He would play games when not totally fit, incredibly during one season whilst suffering from appendicitis, but such was his ability to motivate that he couldn't be left out. Billy Bremner is almost certainly the most famous player ever to pull on the Leeds United shirt.

WE'VE WON IT!

LEEDS UNITED'S CUP HEROES . . . . .

The moment a city had been waiting for . . . Leeds United with the major trophy they have earned so well in beating Arsenal 1-0.

From left to right are Mick Bates, Paul Madeley, Eddie Gray, Paul Reaney, Johnny Giles, Jack Charlton, Allan Clarke, Billy Bremner, Peter Lorimer, Norman Hunter and David Harvey.

. . . AND THE MAN WHO MISSED THIS HISTORIC PICTURE.

Mick Jones, the man with the big heart who made United's goal, ended the match writhing in agony in the Arsenal penalty area.

His elbow had been dislocated in collision with the Arsenal goalkeeper. United trainer Les Cocker told him the match was over and he had a Cup winner's medal as he lay on the turf. He was then carried off on a stretcher, but made a lone brave walk up to the Royal box where the Queen took his hand in both of hers.

The Queen had already handed his medal to another United player and Norman Hunter helped Mick up to the Royal box.

Before his meeting with the Queen, Mick transferred his medal from one hand to the other.

He said later: "I was not going to miss that moment."

Pictured right: Jones attempts to go round Barnett in the run that brought tragedy.

Far right: Barnett and United trainer Les Cocker tend the injured Jones.

And the other hero . . .

This special supplement celebrating United's FA Cup success appeared in the Monday evening *Yorkshire Evening Post* of 8 May 1972. Unfortunately, that night a tired, injury hit United missed out on a deserved 'double' when they were defeated 2-1 at Wolves. There's no doubt that the FA's insistence the game take place within forty-eight hours of the Cup Final affected Leeds' performance. It is doubtful any other team would have received this treatment, such was the strained relationship between the club and FA at the time.

In the 1972/73 season, a potentially successful League campaign floundered when United managed just three wins from their last eleven games and they eventually finished third. As for their defence of the FA Cup, a number of hard-fought victories set up a semi-final clash with Wolves, this Bremner strike being sufficient to take Leeds back to Wembley.

It seemed inconceivable that Leeds could lose to Second Division Sunderland, but Porterfield's first-half strike and Montgomery's heroics in goal saw the Wearsiders hold out for a most unlikely victory. Here, Lorimer is pictured watching in disbelief as Montgomery hurls himself at his point-blank shot to pull off the save of the match.

United left to play AC Milan in Salonika without the suspended Bremner and Clarke or the injured Giles. Leeds had made their debut in the Cup Winners Cup and comfortably reached the final after defeating Ankaragucu, Carl Zeiss Jena, Rapid Bucharest and Hajduk Split. In the final against Milan, Leeds fought valiantly to cancel out their opponents' early disputed goal, but were ultimately unsuccessful. Time and again Leeds were denied by awful refereeing and roughhouse tactics which culminated in Hunter being sent off for retaliation following one challenge too many.

Jack Charlton departs following his last game at the end of the 1972/73 season. Big Jack played a club record 772 matches for Leeds during his twenty seasons, scoring 95 goals. A World Cup winner, he was a tower of strength in defence and created havoc when going forward, especially at set pieces.

Lorimer crashes home a penalty against Birmingham, 8 September 1973. Regarded as being too old by large sections of the media, United confounded their critics by opening the 1973/74 season with seven straight victories (the win against Birmingham was the fifth in the sequence). This was in no small measure due to Revie's ability to motivate, and the team's willingness to drive themselves forward year after year with renewed vigour.

After fourteen games unbeaten Jones scores in the 4-1 success over West Ham on 3 November 1973.

In the final game before Christmas, United wished their fans the season's greetings before a single Terry Yorath goal against Norwich made it twenty-one games unbeaten.

The League run continued into the New Year and the might of Arsenal fell to a rampant Leeds, who had now gone twenty-eight games without defeat. Here, Joe Jordan scores in United's 3-1 win over the Highbury side. However, the pressure was beginning to tell and after a 2-0 triumph at Old Trafford, United were finally defeated by Stoke.

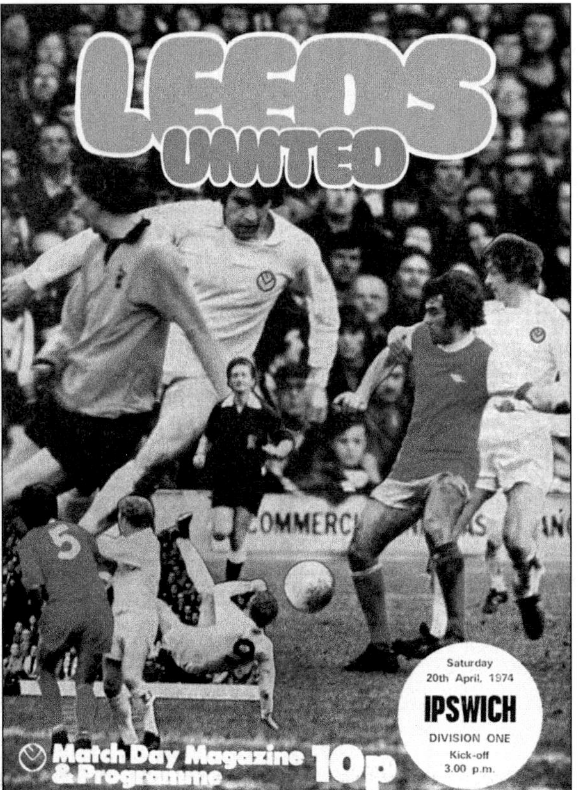

Following their first League defeat results and confidence dipped alarmingly. One victory in seven games found even the most die-hard United fans contemplating another failure. Derby arrived at Elland Road with only six games to go and Leeds were desperate for a victory. 'Commeth the hour commeth the man' – Bremner settled everyone's nerves with this crucial goal in a 2-0 win and United were back on track.

Leeds remained unbeaten until the end of the season, despite squandering a two-goal lead in their penultimate game against Ipswich – fortunately Clarke secured victory with a late winner. This victory ultimately clinched the title for Leeds, because Liverpool failed to defeat Arsenal a few days later.

Leeds United 3 Ipswich Town 2, 20 April 1974. Clarke celebrates his winner with Lorimer as the Kop go wild.

After victory over Ipswich, supporters attempt to secure the last remaining tickets for the final game of the season at QPR on 27 April. On an afternoon of celebration in London, United won with a single Clarke strike.

United acknowledge the adulation of the Kop before Billy Bremner's testimonial match following their Championship success.

The end of an era as Revie and Bremner celebrate the title. Within a couple of months Revie stunned everyone at the club by deciding to accept the vacant post as England manager. Separated, Revie and Leeds would not attain the same heights but together they created artistry and brilliance. Their record during the Revie years was: Division One Champions twice (runners-up five times), FA Cup winners once (runners-up three times), League Cup winners once, Fairs Cup winners twice (runners-up once), Charity Shield winners once, Second Division champions once. In ten seasons in the top flight Leeds always finished in the top four, automatically qualifying for Europe.

Four

Life after Don 1975-1982

Tony Currie, unquestionably the fans' favourite player during the late 1970s.

When Revie left many predicted Johnny Giles would be appointed manager. Controversially the board ignored Giles and chose Brian Clough, known for his outspoken criticism of Leeds. After a turbulent forty-four days Clough was sacked and Jimmy Armfield replaced him. Armfield quickly re-established stability and created an atmosphere which allowed the players to laugh at themselves again. Imagine the verbal abuse Paul Madeley received during this contrived photo-shoot!

The one positive from Clough's short stay was the arrival of Duncan McKenzie. Fans loved his unpredictability and quickness of thought and he soon became a cult hero. However, he was never really given the opportunity to settle in the first team and, despite being top scorer in 1975/76, he left at the end of the season. McKenzie is pictured here performing his party piece at Paul Reaney's testimonial by jumping over a Mini.

Joe Jordan scores in a European Cup first round victory over FC Zurich. After overcoming Ujpest Dozsa and Anderlecht, United found themselves up against Spanish giants Barcelona in the semi-finals. Unsurprisingly, the managerial turmoil had affected Leeds and inconsistent League performances meant they eventually finished ninth, their worst placing since promotion in 1964. It became apparent that success in Europe was all Leeds could hope for.

Leeds won the home leg against Barcelona 2-1 with goals from Bremner and Clarke. The return was a nailbiter of a match. Lorimer's early goal, an equaliser and McQueen's sending-off set up a memorable 'backs to the wall' performance which secured Leeds a place in the final. The players are pictured celebrating Lorimer's strike.

Jordan and Yorath celebrate the result at the Nou Camp. Both players became first team regulars after serving long apprenticeships. Jordan scored 48 goals in his 220 appearances and played 52 times for Scotland, while Yorath scored 12 goals in his 197 games and went on to captain Wales, winning 59 caps in all.

European Cup final, Parc de Prince, 28 May 1975. Even though Revie was only a spectator he must have been bursting with pride as he watched his 'boys' line up for the final against Bayern Munich. From left to right: Stewart, Reaney, Giles, Hunter, F. Gray, Lorimer, Jordan, Madeley, Yorath, Clarke, Hampton, Cherry, E. Gray, Letheran, McKenzie and Bremner.

United fans roar their heroes on before their dream turned into a nightmare.

United's players wait utterly dejected as Bayern receive the trophy. Two incidents turned the match Bayern's way. Firstly, the referee ignored United's penalty appeals following Beckenbaur's blatant foul on Clarke shortly before half-time. Then, on 66 minutes, a linesman ruled out an unstoppable Lorimer volley because Bremner had strayed offside. This latter incident was particularly galling as the referee had initially awarded a goal. United never recovered from these blows and Bayern scored twice on the counter-attack. If the club thought their evening couldn't get worse they were wrong as frustrated Leeds fans rioted, bringing disgrace to the club and a European ban.

McKenzie rises above the Newcastle defence to head home in a 3-0 victory on 9 November 1975. Leeds finished the campaign a creditable fifth. Jimmy Armfield had inherited the hardest task of any Leeds manager in 1975/76 because a fundamental reconstruction of the side was a necessity. Icons such as Bremner, Giles and Hunter needed replacing whilst at the same time he had to satisfy fans expecting nothing less than victory. That he set about it methodically and created an attractive and organised side said much for his managerial ability.

Armfield's best signing was unquestionably Tony Currie. This flamboyant midfielder brightened up every game with his touch, flair and eye for the spectacular. One goal, a twenty-five yard curler against Southampton, was particularly memorable. Sadly, Currie only played 124 times for Leeds, scoring 16 goals.

Gordon McQueen scores United's fourth against Norwich in their 5-2 FA Cup victory in January 1977. 'The Big Scot', a bargain at £30,000, was signed as a long-term replacement for Jack Charlton. A reliable defender, he had a knack of scoring goals from set pieces and eventually played 171 times before following Joe Jordan to Manchester United in February 1978.

Leeds progressed to the fifth round of the FA Cup where they faced Manchester City. In a cracking match a replay at Maine Road seemed inevitable until Trevor Cherry toe-poked this late winner. Unfortunately Leeds missed out on Wembley, falling at the semi-final stage to Manchester United. Cherry played 481 games during a decade at the club and was reliable and consistent, whether in defence of midfield. He played 27 times for England.

Leeds United, 1977/78. From left to right, back row: Hankin, Harris, Cherry, McQueen, Harvey, Stewart, Clarke, Jordan, Currie, Reaney. Front row: Hampton, McNiven, Graham, Lorimer, Gray, Stevenson, Madeley, Gray. The 1977/78 season proved to be Armfield's last as he failed to deliver any silverware. However, in hindsight it is difficult to imagine how any manager could have replaced Revie's ageing squad any better.

Chris Harris evades a QPR defender before getting in a cross during United's 3-0 victory on 3 December 1977. Welsh international Harris was a regular on the right flank and could be a very dangerous forward. After signing for Leeds in 1973 he made a scoring debut in 1975 against Ipswich. However, he was unpredictable and in his 176 games never really fulfilled his potential.

Ray Hankin, seen here scoring in a 3-1 win over Everton on 27 December 1977, arrived as a replacement for Jordan. Initially he produced the goods, top scoring in 1977/78, his first season. However, he couldn't sustain this form and left after scoring 36 times in 103 games.

An appalling day for the club on 3 January 1978. During a third round FA Cup defeat by Manchester City unrest amongst the players boiled over when Harvey and McQueen exchanged blows. This discontent transferred to the crowd and when United conceded a second goal home fans rioted.

When just a single game into the 1978/79 season, Leeds sacked Armfield. Celtic legend Jock Stein took over but only stayed forty-four days before resigning to manage Scotland. The board turned to Jimmy Adamson, who became United's fourth manager since 1974. By mid-November results had improved and Leeds went sixteen League games undefeated and eventually qualified for Europe, having finished fifth. They also reached the League Cup semi-finals, but lost to Southampton after surrendering a two-goal advantage. A key player at this time was left-winger Arthur Graham. Signed in 1978, Graham tormented opponents when in full flight and scored 47 goals in his 260 appearances.

Disappointingly Leeds finished the 1979/80 season in mid-table, mainly due to their inability to score. Embarrassingly, full-back Kevin Hird (first choice penalty taker) was top scorer with 8 goals, the lowest total ever in the club's history. Although the team struggled, a consistent performer, whether at full-back or in midfield, was Frank Gray. Constantly compared to elder brother Eddie, somewhat unfairly, Frank gave excellent service during his two spells, scoring 35 goals in 404 appearances. He is pictured here slotting home a penalty against Bolton in April 1979. He represented Scotland on 32 occasions.

Paul Hart was signed from Blackpool for £300,000 to replace McQueen. After overcoming a difficult start to his Leeds career he went on to play 223 games. In the 1990s he returned to Leeds as part of the coaching staff, and was instrumental in guiding the youth side to their first FA Youth Cup.

Leeds United, 1980/81. From left to right, back row: Madeley, Stevenson, Hart, Lukic, Arins, Firm, Parlane. Middle row: Thomas, Hamson, Connor, Sabella, Adamson (manager), Curtis, Gray, Dickinson, Entwhistle. Front row: Graham, Hird, Chandler, Cherry, Flynn, Harris, Hampton, Burke.

After a terrible start in 1980/81 Leeds replaced Adamson with former hero Allan Clarke, pictured above being welcomed by Eddie Gray and John Lukic in September 1980. Clarke initially concentrated on defence, persuading Eddie Gray to play left-back to assist Hart and Cherry. Leeds recovered to finish ninth, despite scoring only 39 goals. The 1981/82 season started with a 5-1 thumping at Swansea and went downhill from there. The defence leaked goals and the attack only managed 39 again. Clarke bought Peter Barnes for £930,000, but this was a total waste of money as Barnes under-performed. Veteran Frank Worthington, signed in March, scored a few goals but it was too late to save Leeds. A 2-0 defeat at West Brom, amid yet more crowd violence, meant relegation and an end to their longest stay in the First Division – with a total of eighteen years. Left, Clarke is pictured leading Leeds out before a scoreless draw with Manchester United in September 1980.

Five

Wilderness Years 1983-1988

Leeds United, 1984/85. From left to right, back row: Dickinson, Ritchie, McClusky, Linighan, Aspin, Baird. Middle row: Mincher (coach), Hamson, Lorimer, Day, Swinburne, Snodin, Stiles, Ladley (physiotherapist). Front row: Sheridan, Wright, Lumsden (assistant manager), Gray (manager), Gumby (coach), Sellars, Irwin.

When United won only three out of eleven games at the start of the 1985/86 campaign the board sacked Gray. The decision was universally unpopular amongst fans and players. Fans demonstrated and the players met at Leeds solicitors Teeman Levine and issued a statement of condemnation. The board reacted instantly by appointing Billy Bremner manager. Bremner's task was to arrest the club's decline as they hovered close to relegation. Considering defence his priority, Billy sold Ian Snodin for £800,000 to Everton and with the funds purchased Brendon Ormsby and David Rennie to play in front of Mervyn Day. Performances and results began to improve and United finished mid-table.

After five disastrous seasons, 1986/87 proved to be an emotional rollercoaster as United chased an unlikely 'double' of promotion and FA Cup success. The squad was unrecognisable from the team Bremner inherited and this shot shows new-boys Peter Haddock, Jack Ashurst, Ronnie Sinclair, John Buckley, and Russell Doig posing pre-season. Micky Adams, Keith Edwards, John Pearson, Bobby MacDonald and Marc Aizlewood soon joined them at Elland Road. Only Aspin, Day, Ritchie, Baird and Sheridan made the transition from Gray's reign.

Ormsby and Robinson help Ritchie celebrate his goal in a 3-1 victory over Portsmouth. Throughout the 1986/87 campaign Leeds remained around fifth. This was important as play-offs had been instigated to settle the final promotion/relegation place. Goals were not a problem as Ritchie, Edwards, Baird and Sheridan all contributed, and defensively United were consistent, despite one extraordinary 7-2 defeat at Stoke. Seven wins from the last eleven matches clinched fourth spot and a play-off place.

After making his debut in the 1982/83 season, John Sheridan was the star of United's midfield during the 1980s. This free-kick specialist scored 52 goals in his 267 appearances at Leeds and represented the Republic of Ireland on numerous occasions.

In 1986/87 United were involved in an exciting FA Cup run, reaching the semi-finals for the first time in ten years. The top scorer in the season was Ian Baird. A brave centre forward, he loved being in the thick of the action and as a consequence the fans loved him. He made 192 appearances for Leeds, scoring 59 goals. He is pictured here diving between two defenders to put Leeds ahead in their fifth round clash with QPR on 21 February 1987. The match ended 2-1, with Ormsby scoring a late winner.

In their semi-final clash with Coventry, Rennie (11) gave Leeds a shock lead. United contained their First Division opponents until eighteen minutes from time when an Ormsby error gifted Coventry an equaliser. Within minutes Leeds were behind, although Edwards equalised on 86 minutes to send United fans wild and the game into extra-time. Sadly, there was no fairytale ending as Coventry scored the winner.

In the play-off semi-finals United faced Oldham. In the first encounter at Elland Road, amid unbearable tension, Leeds fans had to wait until the final minute for Edwards to give them a slender advantage. Oldham dominated the second leg and deservedly took a two-goal lead with a minute remaining. Incredibly, Leeds went straight down the other end and scored through Edwards – they were now in control thanks to the away goals rule. Leeds held on in extra-time to qualify for the play-off final against First Division Charlton. This photograph shows Ritchie going close against Oldham in the first leg.

With so much at stake the Charlton match provided high emotion and tension and Bremner is pictured acting as peacemaker after an ugly incident almost degenerated into a brawl. Ormsby's second leg goal levelled the scores on aggregate after United's 1-0 defeat at the Valley. The play-off went to a third match at St Andrews.

An exhausted Neil Aspin contemplating his shattered dreams on 29 May 1987. Sheridan had powered home a wonderful free-kick in that decisive game with Charlton to give Leeds the lead with only seven minutes of extra-time remaining. Devastatingly, hopes of a return to the top flight floundered as United were unable to fend off wave upon wave of Charlton pressure and they lost 2-1. It was a shattering end to a season that had promised so much. Aspin, who played 243 times for Leeds, was a hard working defender who always gave his best.

Leeds United, 1988/89. From left to right, back row: Aspin, Ashurst, Grayson, Day, Haddock, Swan, Blake, Rennie. Middle row: Ormsby, Aizlewood, Sheridan, Davison, Sinclair, Williams, Taylor, Maguire, Noteman, Mumby. Front row: Smith, Speed, Pearson, Adams, Snodin, Bremner (manager), Batty, Hilaire, Baird, Stiles, Brockie. A tired and jaded United had begun the 1987/88 season poorly. Despite maximum points from six matches in December they eventually finished seventh, just missing out on the play-offs. In 1988/89 Leeds again started poorly, winning just once by the end of September. Bremner's reign at Leeds was over. It was a sad end to his managerial stint, but to the supporters he will always be 'King Billy'.

Six

'Wilko'

1989-1996

United's only success at Wembley under Howard Wilkinson, 8 August 1992.

Howard Wilkinson watches Gordon Strachan sign for Leeds. The United board had persuaded Howard Wilkinson, manager of Sheffield Wednesday, to drop a division. 'Wilko' immediately raised the players' fitness levels and results improved. Leeds moved out of the relegation zone to finish tenth. Most significantly Wilkinson made a couple of inspirational signings just before transfer deadline day when Chris Fairclough (£500,000 from Spurs) and thirty-two year old Gordon Strachan (£300,000 from Manchester United) joined the club. Strachan could have treated the move as nothing more than a 'paid holiday' after his long and successful career, but this was not Strachan's style and Wilkinson knew it. His energy, boundless enthusiasm, and ability to read the game motivated his teammates. He hated losing and craved success. Without doubt, as Collins and Bremner before him, he was primarily responsible for the rise in the club's fortunes. He would go on to play 243 games for Leeds, scoring 45 goals.

MONDAY, AUGUST 14, 1989.

Yorkshire EVENING POST

Price 20p.

SOCCER SPECIAL

FISTFUL OF HOPE FOR NEW SEASON

LEEDS UNITED new boys Vinny Jones and John McClelland — great mates on and off the field — sum up the determination to bring First Division football back to Elland Road.

The former Wimbledon action man hopes to inspire his new club to achieve the success the loyal Elland Road fans deserve.

And aiming to give him a big helping hand is former Watford defender McClelland in a much che[illegible] United line-up.

Wilkinson knew how to get out of the Second Division and didn't intend hanging around long. Spending over £2 million during the close season, Mickey Thomas, Jim Beglin, Chris O'Donnell, John Hendrie, John McClelland, Mel Sterland, and one surprise – Vinnie Jones from Wimbledon – bolstered his squad. Supporters couldn't wait for the first game of the season as they were convinced promotion was on. Even the *Yorkshire Evening Post* was upbeat about United's prospects in their pre-season *Soccer Special*.

New cult hero Jones shows his skilful side as he heads his first goal for the club against Ipswich on 9 September 1989. After a stuttering start the new signings began to settle and United climbed to the top of the table by Christmas. Crowds increased (at the beginning of the season the average gate was 25,000 and by December it was 30,000) and United were on the march.

Leeds continued to dominate into the New Year and, even though they were nine points clear by February, Wilkinson strengthened his squad. In came strikers Lee Chapman and Imre Varadi and midfielder Chris Kamara. All contributed to arguably the most exciting game of the season against Hull on 10 February 1990. In an action-packed encounter United came from behind to win 4-3, with Varadi and Strachan scoring in the last eight minutes.

Leeds' form dipped after the Hull victory and on 10 March 1990 United arrived at Oxford's Manor Ground without a win in four matches. At the interval Leeds were two goals down but the players showed true fighting spirit, scoring four unanswered goals in the second half. *Above*: Fairclough heads the third goal at Oxford. Fairclough, a brave and intelligent centre-back, scored 8 goals during the campaign, and claimed 23 goals in all during his 240 appearances for Leeds. *Below*: Chapman celebrates scoring United's fourth. United went on to defeat West Ham, Sunderland, and Portsmouth to move ten points clear of Sheffield United. Promotion seemed assured.

As Easter approached United's form dipped again and the chase for promotion intensified with Sheffield United and Newcastle edging unbearably closer. With the pressure on, Leeds looked nervous in their clash with local rivals Bradford City on 7 April 1990. A goal up through Speed, City stole a point with a late penalty. A disgusted Strachan is pictured berating officials for allowing City to take a free-kick from the wrong position – which ultimately led to their penalty.

On 16 April the highest gate of the season (32,727) watched Leeds entertain Sheffield United in a crucial encounter. Fired up, Leeds produced their most clinical form of the season, humiliating their rivals 4-0. The photograph shows Strachan converting from the penalty spot for Leeds' third goal.

Wilkinson and Jones scream out instructions during the home match against Leicester on 28 April 1989. With two games to go the automatic promotion spots had still not been decided. Amid unbearable tension in front of another capacity crowd, Leicester's Gary McAllister equalised Sterland's early goal, before Strachan conjured a miraculous winner on 86 minutes to keep United top.

Leeds travelled to Bournemouth on 5 May 1989 knowing a win would deliver the title, irrespective of other results. On a sweltering Bank Holiday this sole Chapman header, his twelfth goal in 21 appearances, sealed victory. United were back in the top flight!

Leeds parade the Second Division trophy from their open-top bus on the way to a civic reception in May 1989. From left to right: Kamara, Davison, Strachan, Jones and Day.

United's official brochure to mark the 1989/90 Division Two title triumph.

Fairclough heads United's first in a 3-2 triumph at Goodison Park on the opening day of the 1990/91 season. Winning promotion was only the first stage of Wilkinson's plan; the next priority was to ensure United became a force in the top flight rather than also-rans. He strengthened his squad by purchasing Chris Whyte from West Brom, Gary McAllister from Leicester and John Lukic from Arsenal.

Sterland scores United's final goal in a 3-0 victory over Wimbledon in December 1991. United continued to play entertaining football, belying Wilkinson's reputation for producing defensively minded teams who relied too often on the long-ball game. The midfield of Strachan, McAllister, Batty and Speed was gaining a reputation as the best in the League, and Strachan was voted Footballer of the Year. In attack Lee Chapman was simply awesome, scoring 31 goals in all competitions. This was the best return by a United player since John Charles in 1956/57, and his 21 League goals was the best since Peter Lorimer in 1971/72. Leeds finished an impressive fourth and only missed out on a Wembley final when Manchester United beat them in the League Cup semi-finals.

Wilkinson strengthened his squad during the close season before the 1991/92 campaign. New boys David Wetherall, John Newsome, Steve Hodge, Ray and Rod Wallace, and Tony Dorigo pose for cameras.

LEEDS UNITED

THE GLORY SEEKERS

Tuesday 13 August 1991

PUBLISHED BY THE YORKSHIRE EVENING POST, OFFICIAL SPONSOR OF LEEDS UNITED 25P

CHAMPIONSHIP GOAL...Leeds United's midfield star David Batty has the First Division title in his sights this season — and he wouldn't mind scoring the odd goal either.

Evening Post

LEEDS UNITED

INSIDE

Howard Wilkinson's Leeds United side made a huge impression on their return to The Big Time last term.

Now it's all systems go to bring some silverware back to the Elland Road trophy cabinet. Inside this soccer special, published by the *Yorkshire Evening Post*, the club's official sponsor, our experts focus on:

- New boys Tony Dorigo, a £1.3m signing from Chelsea, Steve Hodge, a £900,000 buy from Nottingham Forest, the Wallace twins Rod and Ray who cost a combined fee of £1.7m from Southampton.
- Goal ace Lee Chapman contemplates a repeat of last season's exploits when he was the leading scorer in Division One.
- Midfield terrier David Batty talks about his club and international ambitions for the new season.
- Plus a look at the prospects for Bradford City, Huddersfield Town, Barnsley, Halifax Town, York City and Scarborough plus Yorkshire's top non-league clubs.

The *Yorkshire Evening Post* was confident in its pre-season special.

Early in the season Leeds played Manchester United and earned a well-deserved point in a 1-1 draw at Old Trafford. Chapman is pictured heading United's goal after Schmeichal had misjudged Speed's deep cross.

Having come through the youth system, David Batty was now an established first-team player. Regarded as a defensive midfielder, a Batty goal was rare indeed, so supporters were ecstatic when he scored this one in United's 3-0 win over Manchester City on 7 September 1991. Batty made 256 appearances before his controversial transfer to Blackburn in 1993. Following a spell at Newcastle and numerous England caps he returned to his hometown club for £4.4 million in December 1998.

Leeds were proving to be a hard side to beat and some observers even talked of them being title contenders after hard-earned wins over Chelsea and Liverpool. *Above*: Carl Shutt scores the goal which brought victory at Stamford Bridge. *Below*: This Steve Hodge strike was enough to give United their first win over Liverpool in eighteen seasons.

After their first defeat of the season at Crystal Palace, United responded magnificently with twenty-four points out of a possible twenty-seven to head the table for the first time since 1974. During this run millions of TV viewers witnessed a superb display of attacking football which saw United destroy Aston Villa 4-1 on 24 November 1991. *Above*: Chapman completes a sweeping move with a flying header for United's final goal. *Below*: Ray Wallace's last-minute volley ensured ten-man United defeated Everton 1-0 on 30 November 1991. In his eight seasons at Leeds, Wallace would play 256 matches and score 66 goals, including a Goal of the Season against Tottenham on 17 April 1994. With his pace and skill he proved to be a perfect partner for Chapman.

Over the New Year period Leeds faced Manchester United in the League and both cup competitions. At the end of the 'trilogy' Leeds found themselves out of both cups, but were grateful for this Mel Sterland penalty equaliser that secured a crucial home point on 29 December 1991.

Evening Post

United Review

SHEFFIELD WED. 1
LEEDS UTD 6

Yorkshire Evening Post - Sponsors of Leeds United 1991-92

SIX OF THE BEST

Nice-Lee does it as United back on top

Low dives lift United

MATCH FACTS

LEEDS UNITED

JOHN LUKIC
MEL STERLAND
TONY DORIGO
STEVE HODGE
CHRIS FAIRCLOUGH
CHRIS WHYTE
CARL SHUTT
ROD WALLACE
LEE CHAPMAN
GARY McALLISTER
GARY SPEED

Live TV certainly captured the best of Leeds. Against Sheffield Wednesday at Hillsborough on 12 January 1992 Leeds humiliated their opponents 6-1, with Chapman scoring a glorious hat-trick. This *Yorkshire Evening Post* headline summed up the performance.

After the Sheffield win Leeds' form dipped, due mainly to a Chapman injury. Wilkinson strengthened his attack by signing Eric Cantona, a French striker with a reputation for flare and tantrums. He soon became a cult figure but in reality played only a peripheral role. On 6 April only five games remained with Manchester United a point ahead, having played two games less. However, Leeds kept up the pressure by defeating Chelsea and Coventry, and drawing at Liverpool. Meanwhile, Manchester struggled, and by the end of the Easter programme had gained just five points from as many games: Leeds were now a point ahead. On 26 April 1992 Leeds clinched their first Championship since 1974 when they defeated Sheffield United 3-2 at Bramall Lane, whilst Manchester United lost at Anfield later that day. *Left*: In the encounter with Sheffield, Leeds were a goal behind when Wallace scored an extraordinary 'pinball' equaliser on half-time. McAllister and Speed are pictured congratulating him on his bizarre goal.

In the second half against Sheffield, Leeds had taken the lead though Newsome before the Blades equalised with a Chapman own-goal. With thirteen minutes remaining, Brian Gayle, under pressure from Wallace and Cantona, heads the ball over his advancing 'keeper and into an unguarded net – Leeds were Champions.

'We are the Champions': the *Yorkshire Evening Post* celebrates United's success after clinching the title, 27 April 1992.

PAGE 1

WE ☆ ARE ☆ THE CHAMPIONS

MONDAY APRIL 27 1992 — A YORKSHIRE EVENING POST SPECIAL EDITION — 25P

INSIDE

LEEDS UNITED are the Champions of the Football League for the first time since 1974.

To celebrate this momentous achievement, the *Yorkshire Evening Post* has produced this souvenir special edition.

Inside you'll find bags of news, interviews, statistics and pictures celebrating United's new era of glory.

● Soccer writer DON WARTERS talks to Howard Wilkinson about the season-long quest for the title.

● MIKE CASEY speaks to goalkeeper John Lukic who has just won his second championship.

● There are reports from Bramall Lane and Anfield where the drama which confirmed Leeds as Champions unfolded.

● Plus there are quotes from the rich and famous from inside and outside soccer.

● We look back at United's past campaigns in the European Cup and assess how the whites will fare in next season's competition and MARK DEXTER presents a fan's-eye view of United's championship triumph.

● Our photographers have followed United's exploits throughout the season and there's bags of great pictures capturing United's stars in action.

◄ **WELL PLAYED MATE...** Gary Speed and David Batty congratulate each other on United's victory at Bramall Lane, Sheffield. A few hours later they had even more to celebrate.

The match programme from United's final game of the season against Norwich City, 2 May 1992.

With the title wrapped up, United entertained Norwich in a carnival atmosphere; Wallace scored a superb solo goal to cap a wonderful occasion.

Leeds show off the First Division trophy in front of the Kop, 2 May 1992. From left to right, back row: Chapman, Dorigo, Whyte, McClelland, Lukic, Cantona, Sterland, Batty, McAllister. Front row: Newsome, Hodge, Fairclough, Strachan, Wallace, Speed.

Around 150,000 fans took to the streets for United's victory parade on 3 May 1992.

Eric Cantona scoring the second goal of his hat-trick against Liverpool in the Charity Shield, Wembley, August 1992. In a hugely entertaining match Leeds defeated the Merseysiders 4-3, with goals from Dorigo and Cantona (3). An attacking full-back, Tony Dorigo played 208 matches for Leeds and undoubtedly had the best left foot at the club since Norman Hunter.

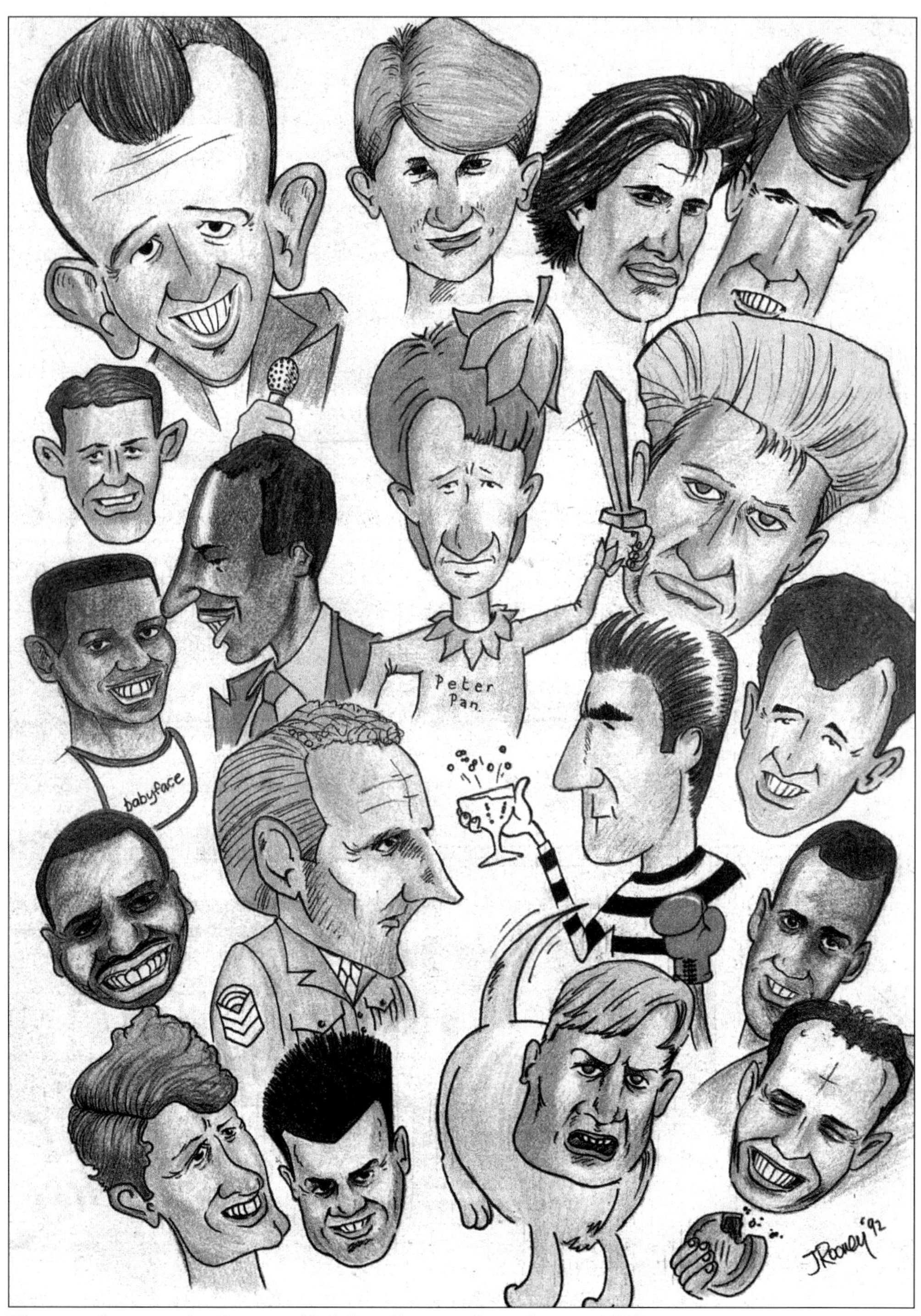

The squad as seen by Rooney, *Yorkshire Evening Post*, August 1992.

Lee Chapman scoring against Sheffield United in October 1992. Although Leeds started the season brightly, losing just once in the opening six fixtures, they found it difficult to string good performances together. Only their home form remained consistent and they stayed unbeaten at Elland Road until December. Chapman was once again top scorer with 17 goals. In total he scored 80 goals in 174 appearances for Leeds, top scoring in three successive seasons from 1990/91 to 1992/93.

In the European Cup first round United were drawn against VFB Stuttgart and allowed themselves to be outplayed and out-thought in the first leg, losing 3-0. Without a hope, and urged on fanatically, United tore into their German opponents in the return leg, destroying them 4-1. So unsettled by the hostile atmosphere were VFB Stuttgart that they inexplicably used an ineligible substitute. As a consequence, and despite losing on aggregate, United were reinstated to play a deciding match at the Nou Camp, Barcelona. One minute after coming on as a second-half substitute, Carl Shutt broke through to give United a 2-1 victory. He is pictured here celebrating his decisive strike. Shutt was always on the fringe of the first team but proved a useful member of the squad, scoring 24 goals in 107 appearances.

OCTOBER 12 1992 26P

BATTLE OF BRITAIN

A YORKSHIRE EVENING POST SPECIAL EDITION

LEEDS UNITED
v
RANGERS

EUROPEAN CUP SECOND ROUND

After defeating Stuttgart, United were drawn to face Rangers in the next round. The media dubbed their clash the 'Battle of Britain'.

In the first leg at Ibrox, United were off to a flying start with this first minute strike from McAllister. Unfortunately, a Lukic blunder and McCoist strike enabled Rangers to edge the tie 2-1. A similar score at Elland Road saw United crash out of the European Cup 4-2 on aggregate.

Wilkinson discusses tactics with his players before extra-time in the FA Cup replay with Arsenal. Leeds had already won a hard fought encounter at Charlton and forced a gutsy draw at Highbury to get to this stage. Unfortunately, in a thrilling game Leeds went down by the odd goal in a five.

Gordon Strachan scores one of the goals that made up his hat-trick against Blackburn on 10 April 1993. In reality the 1992/93 season, which had promised so much, almost had a disastrous conclusion as United struggled throughout to play like defending Champions. As the season drew to a close Leeds found themselves on the fringes of the relegation battle and their last win of the campaign, a 5-2 triumph over Blackburn, came with six matches still to play. Safety was only achieved in the penultimate fixture at Sheffield Wednesday when they drew 1-1. Leeds had the dubious honour of becoming the first defending Champions to be unable to win an away League game all season.

Leeds United, 1993/94. From left to right, back row: Ray Wallace, Newsome, Strandli, Wetherall, Beeney, Lukic, McAllister, Deane, Hodge. Middle row: Hennigan (trainer), O'Leary, Whelan, Tinkler, Sharp, Kelly, Rocastle, Fairclough, Dorigo, Sterland, Ladley (physiotherapist). Front row: Speed, Kerslake, Batty, Wilkinson (manager), Strachan, Forrester, Rod Wallace. After below par performances the previous season, Wilkinson freshened up his squad. His purchases included Sheffield United's Brian Deane for £2.7 million, as a replacement for Chapman, and David O'Leary on a free from Arsenal to add experience to the defence. Mel Sterland and Chris Whyte, members of the 1992 title-winning side, departed having each played 146 games.

The Leeds players celebrate Deane's goal at Southampton on 11 September 1993. United finally vanquished their away-day blues in the fourth away game of the 1993/94 season with a 2-0 win at Southampton, Speed scoring the other goal. The result galvanised United, who went a further eighteen games with just a single defeat.

United were involved in many entertaining games during the 1993/94 season, including four-goal thrashings of Wimbledon and Chelsea, and back-to-back 3-3 draws with Blackburn and Sheffield Wednesday. On 4 December 1993 Leeds defeated Manchester City 3-2, Deane scoring this late winner. Deane played with heart and fire but struggled to score consistently throughout his Leeds career. In all he totalled 38 goals in 168 appearances.

Overall the 1993/94 season was successful for Leeds, despite missing out on Europe by one place. New skipper Gary McAllister was at his peak: stylish and an expert at dead-ball situations, his maturing performances won him the Scottish captaincy. This photograph shows him firing home against Everton on 30 April 1994.

Wetherall celebrates his goal against Manchester United with Kelly and Wallace; Leeds won this match 2-1 on 11 September 1994. Three years after winning the title Wilkinson had reshaped his side. New signings included Carlton Palmer, John Pemberton, Phil Masinga and Lucas Radebe. Youngsters from the reserves and the 1993 Youth Cup winning team included Wetherall, Kelly, Whelan, Ford and Forrester. The new team made an encouraging start when the 1994/95 season began, winning three of the opening five matches. Gary Kelly became a regular for both Leeds and the Republic of Ireland. Currently Kelly is United's second longest serving player after David Batty and his appearances would undoubtedly have been higher had he not missed the entire 1998/99 season through injury.

United's form was erratic during the 1994/95 campaign and Wilkinson took a gamble and signed Tony Yeboah from Eintracht Frankfurt on loan. Immediately United's League form improved to such an extent they pipped Newcastle for the last European spot on the final day of the season, drawing 1-1 at Tottenham. Yeboah was the star, making an immediate impact with 12 goals in his 18 appearances. He is pictured here celebrating his hat-trick against Ipswich.

Yeboah, top scorer in both 1994/95 and 1995/96, started the season sensationally, scoring 11 goals in the opening 9 games (including hat-tricks against Monaco and Wimbledon). He also scored this unstoppable volley against Liverpool – which proved to be the Goal of the Season – on 21 August 1995.

After this bright start United's League form began to disappoint, due mainly to the loss of Yeboah through injury. However, an early exit in the UEFA Cup to PSV Eindhoven did not prevent Leeds performing well in both domestic cup competitions. This photograph shows Deane scoring United's final goal in their 5-1 aggregate victory over Birmingham in the League Cup semi-finals. United had reached a Wembley final for the first time since 1973.

McAllister tries in vain to create an opening against Villa at Wembley in the League Cup final. Unfortunately, all hopes of winning silverware in 1995/96 evaporated during one week in March. Firstly, Liverpool defeated United in an FA Cup sixth round replay at Anfield, then a few days later at Wembley Leeds fell apart against Aston Villa and were humiliated 3-0, their worst performance for years. United fans blamed Wilkinson for this defeat and felt betrayed by his selection policy and tactics. A miserable run to the end of the season fuelled discontent amongst supporters.

A distraught Wilkinson watches his side being outclassed by Manchester United, September 1996. Prior to the 1996/97 season, Caspian Group plc purchased Leeds United and a new managing director, Peter Ridsdale, was appointed. With fresh funds available new players arrived, most significantly Nigel Martyn and Lee Bowyer. Meanwhile, Speed, McAllister and Lukic (after 430 games) departed from the club. During their time at Leeds both Speed and McAllister had scored on a regular basis from midfield. Speed had the slightly better record of 57 goals in 311 matches, compared to McAllister's 45 in 294. Rumours were still circulating that Howard Wilkinson was about to be replaced by George Graham and gossip became fact when Leeds were thrashed 4-0 at home by Manchester United. Within forty-eight hours Wilkinson was sacked and another forty-eight hours later George Graham was appointed manager. Although many fans at the time celebrated his departure, nothing can devalue Wilkinson's achievements. In less than four years he transformed a club floundering in the Second Division into one that won the First Division title. Leeds also visited Wembley twice and finished in the top five on four occasions. Perhaps just as importantly, Wilkinson left as his legacy a youth policy about to mature.

Seven

The Move Towards Youth 1997-1999

Harry Kewell, arguably the Leeds United Academy's star pupil.

All supporters desperate for a return to the good times welcomed Graham's arrival. Despite his questionable 'off the field' activities, which earned him a ban following the infamous FA 'bung' inquiry, Graham's management credentials were first rate. His initial task was to avoid relegation at all cost. Entertainment went out of the window as he built his team from defence, grinding out result after result. Leeds finished mid-table and scored the fewest goals (28) in the League. Graham believed that too many of the existing squad were 'showboating prima donnas' and out went Yeboah, Brolin, Palmer and Rush and in came new signings Robert Molenaar and Gunnar Halle.

In his first season at the club Nigel Martyn was voted Player of the Year. Consistently reliable, he kept 23 clean sheets and forced his way back into the England squad. By the end of the 1998/99 campaign he had already played 132 games for United.

A major plus for the club during the 1996/97 season was the youth team's 'double' triumph of Northern Intermediate League and FA Youth Cup, the latter being the second time the club had won that competition in four seasons.

Budding United stars show off the FA Youth Cup after their triumph over Crystal Palace, 3-1 on aggregate, 15 May 1997. Included in this group are Harry Kewall, Stephen McPhail, Matthew Jones, Alan Maybury, Paul Robinson, Jonathon Woodgate and Lee Matthews.

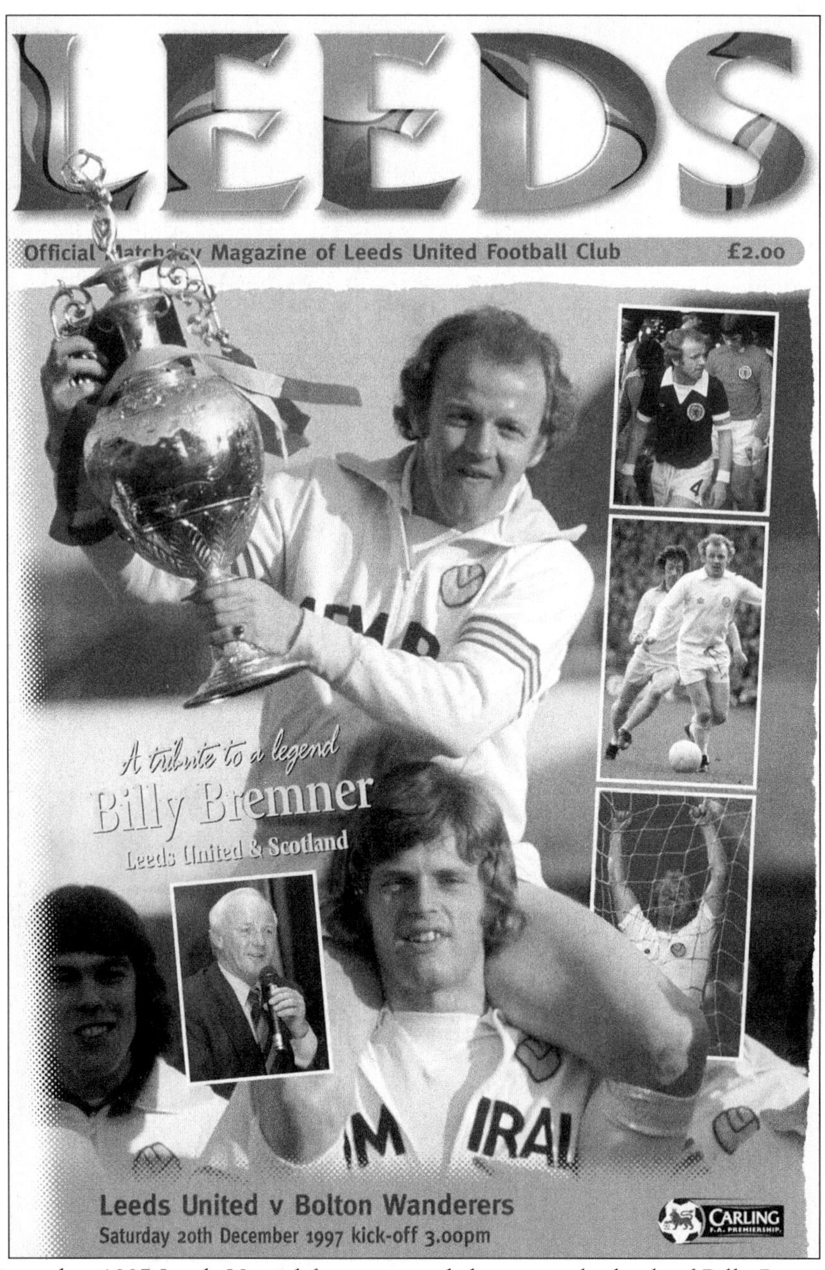

On 7 December 1997 Leeds United fans mourned the untimely death of Billy Bremner, aged just fifty-four. Rather than ineptly articulate his relationship with the club in our words, we would prefer to reproduce some of his own feelings for the club that he gave to us during the writing of our book, *Leeds United Cup Kings 1972*. 'If I had my time again I wouldn't change anything; I just loved playing. I used to think I'm lucky I can play a game that I get paid for, that I would do for nothing. The biggest thing for me was to be able to play with a bunch of guys that got on well with each other over the long period of time we were together. We only knew Leeds United and we loved Leeds United. Many of us had never heard of the club before we came, so to actually grow up and love that club and to have those same feelings today is tremendous. The biggest thrill I ever had was wearing the white shirt of Leeds United.'

Within a year of Graham taking charge United had a new-look squad. At the start of the 1997/98 season the general feeling amongst supporters and media alike was that Leeds were once again moving in the right direction.

Graham's new signings parade before the cameras prior to the start of the season. From left to right: Dennis Lilley, Jimmy 'Floyd' Hasselbaink, David Hopkin, David Robertson, Bruno Ribeiro, Pierre Laurent, and Alfie Haaland.

'Jimmy' scores on his debut against Arsenal on 8 August 1997. Totally unpredictable, Hasselbaink could whinge and whine with the best of them, yet possessed an explosive shot and terrified opposing defenders when running at them. Top-scorer in 1997/98 and 1998/99, he scored 42 goals in 87 appearances for Leeds before succumbing to the lure of the peseta, joining Athletico Madrid for a club record fee of £12 million in August 1999.

What a difference a season makes! Wetherall celebrates his winning goal against Manchester United in September 1998. Wetherall stayed seven seasons with Leeds before leaving at the end of the 1998/99 campaign. A solid defender, he played 250 games and scored 18 goals.

In comparison to the previous season, the most significant change in United's tactics in 1997/98 was their willingness to attack, making Leeds one of the Premiership's most exciting teams to watch. Derby were the team to suffer most as Leeds completed a remarkable 'double' over the Midlands club. *Above*: Bowyer celebrates his last-minute winner as United complete a spectacular comeback at Elland Road, winning 4-3 after trailing by three goals, 8 November 1997. *Below*: Halle scores in the return fixture at Pride Park where Derby were buried 5-0 by a sparkling Leeds performance.

Leeds United will always be indebted to Captain John Hackett's split second decision to abort the take-off of his plane carrying United's squad back from a match with West Ham on 30 March 1998. His decisive action unquestionably saved the lives of all the passengers on board, who unbelievably escaped from this wreckage with only minor injuries. Though clearly shaken by the experience United finished the season fifth, high enough for them to qualify for Europe. All things considered, the 1997/98 season was successful, despite the disappointment of United's failure to beat Wolves in the sixth round of the FA Cup at Elland Road.

United's youth policy continued to prosper as many of the FA Youth Cup side, nurtured by Eddie Gray, formed the backbone of the side that won the Pontins League First Divison title for the first time in sixty-one years on 7 May 1998.

United's poor start to the 1998/99 campaign was due mainly to George Graham's messy, drawn out departure to Tottenham, and the handling of David O'Leary's wish to succeed him. O'Leary was eventually offered the post after United were continually frustrated in their attempts to bring Leicester's Martin O'Neill to Elland Road. O'Leary only agreed to become manager if substantial funds were made available to back his judgement on new signings – the board were as good as their word. This photograph shows a delighted Ridsdale and O'Leary presenting their first signing, David Batty, to the media. With Wallace having departed pre-season, this left Batty as the final link with United's 1992 Championship team.

Howard Wilkinson had signed Lucas Radebe, seen here in action against Sheffield Wednesday, in the summer of 1994 from Kaizer Chiefs. Radebe recovered from a cruciate knee ligament injury to become a world class centre half. Captain of both club and country, few players in modern day football can read the game, tackle and distribute as well as he can.

Prior to United's 3-1 victory at Liverpool the managerial shenanigans appeared to have ruined the season before it had even started. Already out of the UEFA Cup and Worthington Cup, United were going nowhere. The Anfield victory galvanised Leeds into a number of stirring performances, aided by the introduction of a number of talented youngsters who were given – and proved able to take – their opportunity. *Above*: Seventeen year old substitute Alan Smith slots home a debut goal within minutes of coming on at Anfield. *Below*: Eighteen year old Jonathon Woodgate in action against Derby County. Woodgate ended a remarkable first season being capped by England.

Leeds equalled their top-flight club record (set in 1973) of seven successive League victories when they defeated Nottingham Forest 3-1 on 3 April 1999. This superb sequence of results epitomised just how far the team had come in so short a period of time under O'Leary and assistant manager Eddie Gray.

SATURDAY NIGHT RESULTS EDITION

GREEN FINAL

YORKSHIRE SPORT

BEST REPORTS ON THE TOP MATCHES

LEEDS UNITED	3-1	YORK CITY	1-2
BARNSLEY	2-1	SCARBORO'	Late
BRADFORD C	3-0	MIDDLESBRO'	0-0
HUDDS TOWN	1-1	HALIFAX T	2-2

SATURDAY & SUNDAY 3 & 4 APRIL 1999 — YS/93911 45P

IT'S A KNOCK-OUT READ EVERY WEEK

YORKSHIRE'S BIG FIGHT PREVIEW: CENTRE PAGES

7TH HEAVEN

United equal record run of wins

SUPER Leeds Unite[d] equalled a record that ha[s] stood for a quarter of [a] century as they beat Not[t]ingham Forest 3-1 a[t] Elland Road today.

• Match report: Page 3

• ROCKET MAN: Jimmy Hasselbaink blasts the ball into the net to put Leeds United on the way to a record-equalling victory. PICTURE: CHARLES KNIGHT

WIN LEEDS UNITED TICKETS: SEE PAGE 31

The *Green Final* describes United's record equalling feat.

Goal-maker Kewall congratulates goalscorer Hasselbaink after his late goal in the 1-0 win over Arsenal in the final home game of the 1998/99 season. United finished fourth and qualified for Europe once again – a wonderful achievement for such a young squad. With observers of the game eulogising the potential of O'Leary's side, the club's eightieth year could hardly have ended any brighter. How can any Leeds fan not be looking forward to the next chapter in the Leeds United story?